BOB ACTO

AROUN
ST AGNES &
PERRANPORTH

Round Walks
from Holywell to Porthtowan

This fully revised version of *A View from St Agnes Beacon*
first published 1994 by
LANDFALL PUBLICATIONS
Landfall, Penpol, Devoran, Truro, Cornwall TR3 6NW
Telephone: Truro (0872) 862581.

MY THANKS TO ....

Leslie Douch, former Curator of the County Museum, Truro, and the
leading authority on East Wheal Rose, for checking my typescript of Walk
1; Margaret Bunt, Isobel Hedges and Philip Childs for information about St
Agnes and the loan of useful books; Gill Jacobs for providing me with a
sort of "Which? Guide to the Best Pubs and Other Places of Refreshment" in
the area; Kenneth Brown for information on mines; Roger Glanville and
Ron Grubb for sharing their knowledge of Rose and district with me; and
several members of the St Agnes Museum Trust, but above all the
Secretary, Roger Radcliffe, who meticulously corrected my inaccuracies in
both editions and supplied dozens of extra points of interest. I am grateful,
too, to the many authors whose books have helped me - mainly those listed
at the back - and to all the people I met en route or have chatted to over the
telephone, who supplied innumerable useful "snippets". Finally, as always,
I want to thank my wife, Viv, not only for providing ideas, information,
and companionship on the walks, but also for putting up with being
disturbed frequently in the wee small hours when I got up to draw another
picture or type a few more pages.

PLEASE NOTE .....

All these walks are, to the best of my knowledge, on public rights of way.
For your own safety, keep to the official paths in mining areas and on
clifftops. If you take a good torch on the walks, you will have several
opportunities to explore mineshafts and caves, but please take great care:
roof-falls are not unknown, and tides have a nasty habit of coming in.....

Typesetting, maps and illustrations by Bob Acton.
Printed by the Troutbeck Press
and bound by R. Booth Ltd., Mabe, Penryn, Cornwall.

CONTENTS

INTRODUCTION 4

WALK 1 St Newlyn East & East Wheal Rose *(About 3 miles)* . . . 5

WALK 2 Ventongimps, Callestick & the Chiverton
         Mines *(About 4½ or nearly 6 miles)* 12

WALK 3 Bolingey, New Chiverton, Wheal Albert
         & St Piran's Round *(About 7 miles)* 19

WALK 4 Perranzabuloe Church, Bolingey
         & Penwartha Coombe *(About 3 miles)* 27

WALK 5 Holywell, Ellenglaze, St Piran's Oratory & Penhale Point
         with an optional extension to Cubert *(About 8 or 9 miles)* . . 32

WALK 6 Perranporth, Perran Sands, St Piran's Oratory
         & Rose *(About 4½ or 5 miles)* 45

WALK 7 Perranporth, Perrancoombe, Mithian, Trevellas
         Coombe & the Coast *(About 7½ miles)* 51

WALK 8 Porthtowan, Mingoose & Chapel Porth *(About 6½ miles)* . . 61

WALK 9 In and around St Agnes Village *(About 3 miles)* 71

WALK 10 St Agnes, Newdowns Head, Chapel Porth &
         St Agnes Beacon *(About 6 miles, or a shorter alternative)* . . 83

SOME MINING TERMS USED IN THIS BOOK 92

FURTHER READING 95

INTRODUCTION

This book aims to provide a selection of round walks which can be enjoyed by all, and at the same time to give information about the interesting details along the way. The main focus is on the old mines and associated industries such as mineral railways, and there are few areas in Cornwall, or indeed in the world, where the surviving evidence of these things is more plentiful and spectacular. Other features of the area covered - that is, from Holywell westwards as far as Porthtowan, and inland as far as St Newlyn East and Chyverton House - are also included in the directions and italicised notes, such as the churches, famous local people, and ancient archaeological sites.

Using the Book

Before you set off, please read the introductory remarks for the walk in question, which will give you some hints about such things as the sort of footwear needed, and whether you will be able to find refreshments on the walk. In some cases, too, you could increase the pleasure of the walk by making prior arrangements, such as telephoning for permission to visit certain sites.

Directions are given in **bold type**, and the symbol (*) refers you to an *italicised note*. On pages 92-4 there is a glossary explaining the mining terms used in the book.

The book has a waterproof cover and will fit easily when open into the sort of clear polythene bag used in supermarkets to wrap fruit and vegetables ..... so there's no need for rainy weather to prevent you from doing the walks. The sketch maps are not drawn to scale, and give only a rough idea of the route, but you should be in no danger of going astray if you follow carefully the very detailed directions. Even so, if you can take along the relevant Ordnance Survey Landranger or Pathfinder map your understanding of what you see will be further enhanced, and you will have the opportunity to explore this splendid region for yourself.

NOTE TO THE SECOND EDITION

This is a considerably enlarged version of *A View from St Agnes Beacon*. Bigger is not always (perhaps not even usually) better, but with the help of many well-informed and generous people I hope and believe genuine improvements have been made, in the presentation as well as the content of the book. If not, I'm sure it won't be long before my regular readers (and walkers, of course) let me know. I await their response with interest.

Bob Acton

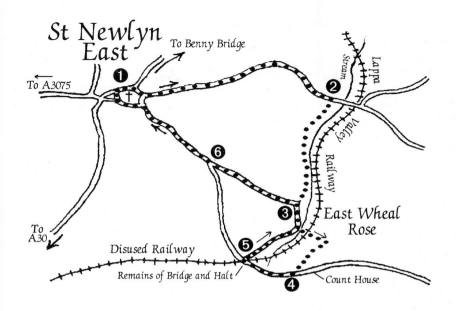

WALK 1

ST NEWLYN EAST & EAST WHEAL ROSE

About 3 miles

East Wheal Rose was in its day the most important lead mine in Cornwall, and the ruined engine house is the largest and among the most impressive in the County. It stands on land owned by the Lappa Valley Railway, and between Easter and the end of September you can visit the site by being a passenger on the miniature railway which runs (between 10.15 a.m. and 5.30 p.m. every day, including Sundays) from the station at Benny Bridge, which is not on the walk route. Outside that period access to the site is only by permission of the owner, Mrs Dani Booth, who tells me she loves walking herself and would not want to deny anyone genuinely interested in East Wheal Rose the chance to inspect it. If you wish to do so, please phone her, preferably several days in advance, on Mitchell 510643.

The walk suggested, which gives you a fairly distant, but still impressive, view of the mine buildings, is quite a short one, including country roads and a most attractive valley path beside a stream. Parts of the path are likely to be muddy.

Shops are available at St Newlyn East, and the Peacock, near the church, offers good bar food.

To drive to St Newlyn East from St Agnes, take the B3285 to Goonhavern via Perranporth. At Goonhavern turn left on to the Newquay road (A3075), and after about three miles turn right, just past Rejerrah. To drive from Truro, you first need to get to the A30. You could use the main roads (A390 westwards and turn right at Chiverton Cross, or A3076 north and turn left at Carland Cross), but pleasanter would be to go up Kenwyn Road and follow the B3284 as far as Shortlanesend, there forking right on to a minor road to join the A30 south of Zelah. Turn right, and about a mile past Zelah fork left, signposted Newlyn East. After another mile turn right, as signposted. In the village, turn right at the T-junction. You should find room to park near the church (*).

ST NEWLYN EAST CHURCH

St Newlyna's church dates from the 13th century. The fig tree growing out of its south wall is said to have sprung up when she struck the ground with her staff, saying, "Let a church be built." (Manaccan church, near Helford, boasts a similarly surprising fig.) Please treat the tree with care: anyone who harms it is doomed to die within a year. The saint herself, who may be the same person as the Saint Noluen, patron of Noyale Pontivy in Brittany, is supposed to have met an untimely end by beheading; a 15th-century Lantern Cross near the font portrays a woman holding her head in her arms. Parts of the chancel and north transept, plus the font, are Norman, and the aisles seem to be 14th- and 15th-century workmanship. The tower was added in the 15th century. The old bench ends at the front of the nave remain, and parts of the medieval rood screen were incorporated in the new one when the church was restored in 1883 - a restoration which, unusually, earns John Betjeman's approval in "Cornwall: A Shell Guide". Under the church is a vault

The fig-tree in winter

in which were laid to rest seventeen members of the Arundell family, whose nearby Tudor manor house, Trerice, is now owned by the National Trust, and is a "must" for all visitors to this area. "Around Newquay" includes a walk based on Trerice.

❶ Approaching the church from the T-junction, turn left. At the next T-junction, the Pheasant Inn faces you; here turn right, and then fork right along Metha Road, ignoring the left turning signposted to Trerice. 150 years ago the old cottages on Metha Road were mostly occupied by miners, who were granted the privilege of keeping animals on Newlyn Downs. According to the WI's book of Cornish villages, the right to do so still appears on the deeds of these cottages. **After a little over half a mile, this attractive country road dips into the Lappa Valley, and you take the footpath on the right, signposted to Nanhellan** - but first it's worth continuing downhill for another hundred yards to Metha Bridge, where there are in fact two bridges, the second being over what was originally a mineral railway built by J. T. Treffry (*). It later became part of the G.W.R., and is now the Lappa Valley miniature steam railway.

TREFFRY'S MINERAL RAILWAY

Joseph Thomas Treffry (pronounced to rhyme with "reply") was one of Cornwall's most daring and imaginative entrepreneurs. His main business interests were in the St Austell china-clay area, and he built Par harbour; his viaduct-cum-aqueduct in the Luxulyan valley is most spectacular. (See "Around St Austell" and "Around the River Fowey" for walks exploring these.) In 1837 he bought a small village on the north coast, named after a "new quay" which had been built at least as far back as the 15th century. He developed Newquay's harbour and built a railway for horse-drawn wagons to connect it with his clay pits near St Dennis. In 1849 an extension was added, to East Wheal Rose. In 1873 these "tramways" were bought up by the Cornwall Minerals Railway, converted for use by steam locomotives, and this branch was extended to Treamble to serve the iron mines there: see Walk 5. But there was less demand for the railway's services than had been expected, and before long the lines were taken over by the Great Western Railway in order to complete their route from Chacewater to Newquay. The Treamble branch was used during World War II for troop movements to and from Penhale Camp at Holywell. The Chacewater-Newquay line was eventually axed by Beeching in the 1960s. Unfortunately, the chance to convert it into an attractive footpath was missed. Lewis Reade's "Branch Line Memories" contains a special feature on the Chacewater to Newquay branch line. Since so many of the walks in this book follow or cross its former track, reading his account and studying his photographs would, I'm sure, enhance your enjoyment. His later volume, devoted entirely to Cornwall, is also worth having.

❷ Return to the footpath, which runs beside the stream - very close to it in places, so you must expect mud underfoot. It is also rather uneven, and a little scrambling is needed here and there. This is a lovely wooded valley, a carpet of bluebells in May and of leaves in the late autumn. Although the water in the stream always seems to be clear, the bed has the kind of reddish tinge I associate with deposits of ochre, as seen for example in the Carnon River between Twelveheads and Bissoe. Soon after the old quarry you have a good view of the stack and engine house of East Wheal Rose (*). **You cross stone and wooden stiles, and then the path curves right. Go through the six-bar metal gate and up the farm track to the road.**

The house and stack for the great 100-inch engine, as they were in 1989

EAST WHEAL ROSE

East Wheal Rose is one of the few Cornish mines to have had a whole book devoted to it: see the Further Reading list. The maps, diagrams and photographs it contains, as well as Leslie Douch's fascinating account of the mine's history, would add greatly to your enjoyment of this walk. All I can attempt here is to point to a few of the basic facts. There were already old workings on a site about two miles west (marked Deer Park Mine on the O.S. Pathfinder map) when exploratory shafts were sunk in 1812, and it was at once clear that the sett was rich in silver as well as lead. Soon, John Giddy, an employee at the tin-smelting works at Calenick (see "A Second View from Carn Marth", Walk 12) was brought in to manage the mine and set up a lead-smelting house. A residence was built for him at Shepherds, south west of Fiddlers Green. By 1823 the enterprise was making a good profit, but as the shafts went deeper, the quantity and quality of both lead and silver declined. So did the price of lead, and Old Wheal Rose was abandoned at the end of 1832. A new venture started further east, in the valley of the little River Lappa, in 1834; this proved very productive. "Today," writes Douch, "it is difficult to imagine the scene in the valley when the boom was at its height and the transformation of a quiet stream bed where nothing more mechanical than a water-mill had worked - to the clatter and noise, the hissing and blowing,

8

the bustle and seeming confusion of East Wheal Rose, with over a thousand men, women and children at work, wagons rolling in laden with timber and coals, rolling out with lead ore for the local smelters or the ports, the adit water running heavy and red right down to the Gannel (Newquay)." In July 1846 *occurred a disaster, the worst in Cornish mining history: 38 miners drowned when a cloudburst flooded the workings. (Detailed and harrowing accounts of what happened are included by Alan Bennett in "Images of Cornwall" and Cyril Noall in "Cornish Mine Disasters".) The mining was always difficult: the lode was so soft that in 1850 the Mining Journal described it as "literally a quicksand"; "a complete forest of Norway fir has been stowed away underground" to support the shafts. In 1857, the same journal called East Wheal Rose "an exceedingly dangerous (mine) in which to work, probably the most so in the world." The coming of Treffry's tramroad in 1849 helped to revive the mine's fortunes, but production declined, and the expense of pumping increased as the levels grew deeper, so despite evidence of very rich lead deposits below the 170-fathom level, the underground mining stopped in 1857, although metal went on being recovered profitably from the halvans. Most of the buildings that housed engines during the 1840s and '50s were on the site now covered by the landscaped rubbish tip. In 1881, new adventurers set about mining the deeper ore, and they put to work a very big pumping engine (a new 90-inch one manufactured by Harvey & Co. of Hayle) at Penrose's Shaft; the splendid ruins of the base of its engine house stand on high ground a little way south of this walk route. At about the same time the most powerful beam engine ever to work in Cornwall (which had a cylinder 100 inches in diameter, and had been made, also by Harvey's, for Great Wheal Vor, west of Helston, in 1853) was purchased and installed in a magnificent new engine house at North Wheal Rose Shaft, with a chimney 100 feet high beside it. (Perhaps the height of the stack was symbolic.) The bob (beam) alone of the engine weighed 55 tons. The cost of all the new machinery was never recovered, and in 1885, just before the crucial 170-fathom level was reached, East Wheal Rose finally closed. The 100-inch engine, which had worked in Wales before coming here, was sold and taken to Millom in Cumbria. The engine house itself now belongs to a local educational trust, which has the responsibility of maintaining it. My original note in the first edition of this book ended as follows: "Mrs Booth, the owner of the miniature railway, tells me that the last remnants of the roof fell in during spring 1988, and that there are many other signs of deterioration; urgent action would seem to be needed to preserve this building, which is surely of national importance." I am delighted to be able to add that such action has now been taken.*

❸ **Turn left. Soon you pass the ancient-looking farmhouse, Nanhellan. About a hundred yards after that, take the public footpath on the left signposted to East Wheal Rose.** It leads to a footbridge and then to what was, when I wrote "A View from St Agnes Beacon", a vast refuse tip. Since then it has been closed to further dumping, and landscaped so successfully that it's hard to imagine now the ugliness and desolation that so recently characterised this area. A wooden fence on the left discourages trespass in that direction, tempting though that may be for those who want a closer view of the great engine house; **the right of way continues almost straight ahead, up the steep slope that marks the edge of the old waste tip, and across the field at the top.** A second change affecting the place since I originally researched this walk is nearly as dramatic as the first: it results from the creation of a "wind farm" at Carland Cross. The tall windmills, though a mile away, dominate the view, and on the day I last did this walk the breeze carried to my ears a constant sound as of a distant stormy sea. **Head slightly to the left of the windmills. As you start to go downhill, look out for a wooden post marked with yellow arrows on the edge of the strip of woodland below. Go down to that and then turn right. The path runs in the hollow along the edge of the wood and eventually joins the road at a stile on the right-hand side of a pair of large metal gates - once the main entrance to the tip.**

❹ Turn right at the road. Soon you cross the stream again; the red tinge to its bed is still apparent, and the big area of old mine workings from which it flows here may well provide the explanation. Next come the remains of a bridge which carried the old railway, and the small path up the bank on the left on the far side leads (though a wooden fence now bars access) to a tiny platform, a melancholy monument to Dr Beeching. This was once Mitchell and Newlyn Halt - "a railway archaeology site well worth a visit," as Lewis Reade says.

❺ Turn right just beyond the railway bridge, along a narrow road heading towards East Wheal Rose engine house. Keep to this road as it bends left at Nanhellan, then runs uphill between high hedges.

❻ At the T-junction (Ventonarren Farm) turn right. This, for the reason you now know, is called Halt Road, and it soon brings you back to St Newlyn East church.

If you want to take a trip on the miniature railway and inspect the mine buildings at close quarters, drive or walk up the road signposted to Trerice, which is the left turn near the start of the walk I have described. The railway terminus is at Benny Bridge.

East Wheal Rose 100-inch engine house before the ivy was removed

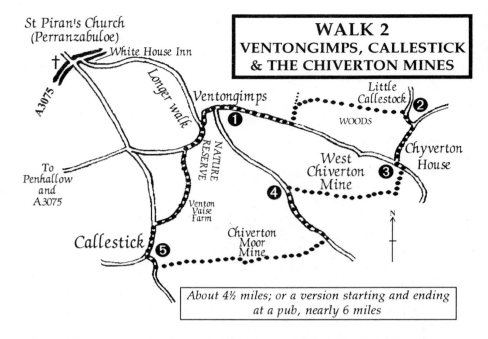

St Piran's Church
(Perranzabuloe)

White House Inn

A3075

Longer walk

Ventongimps

①

To
Penhallow
and
A3075

NATURE RESERVE

Venton
Vaise
Farm

Callestick **⑤**

Chiverton
Moor
Mine

Little
Callestock **②**

WOODS

Chyverton
House

West
Chiverton
Mine **③**

④

N

WALK 2
VENTONGIMPS, CALLESTICK
& THE CHIVERTON MINES

*About 4½ miles; or a version starting and ending
at a pub, nearly 6 miles*

West Chiverton's engine house is just as unusual as that of East Wheal Rose, and almost as imposing; it illustrates well the builders' pride in their work. The walk also includes the remains of a smaller lead mine, and passes through the beautiful estates of Chyverton House. You could visit the famous gardens (by prior arrangement: see the directions), and also inspect a nature reserve at Ventongimps. About half of the route is on very quiet roads; the rest is tracks and paths through woodland and open fields. There are muddy patches. Just west of Little Callestock you may have some barbed wire to negotiate, and soon after passing Chiverton Moor Mine you will need to be careful not to miss the correct path; but you are unlikely to have any serious difficulties. There is no shop on this walk, as far as I know, but the longer route starts and ends at an inn which does good food. At Callestick you could visit Callestock Cider Farm to sample their scrumpy and find out about the art of cider making.

The shorter version of this walk starts and ends at Ventongimps. To drive there from St Agnes, take the B3285 (Perranporth) road. After less than two miles turn right on to minor roads which take you through Mithian to join the A3075 (Newquay) road just south of Penhallow. Turn left and then first right. To drive from Truro, take the A390 westwards; at the big Chiverton roundabout, where it meets the A30, turn right on to the A3075 Newquay road. At Penhallow, about three miles further on, turn right for Ventongimps. There is not much room to park in the village. If you turn right, over the bridge and past the old watermill, you may find space on the left after a few yards, but please avoid blocking any entrances. A little further up, the road widens somewhat just before a house on the left, and this is probably the best spot for a parked car or two.

For the longer version, continue along the A3075 to Perranzabuloe; the church is on the left, and on the right is the White House Inn, whose owners have kindly given me permission to suggest that you park there. The Inn is noted for good food, so it makes an ideal ending for a walk. It stands at a corner where a country road joins the A3075; to start from there, walk along this quiet road. After about half a mile it brings you to Ventongimps. Turn left over the bridge.

VENTONGIMPS

The name means "level spring" (Cornish, fenten compes); Oliver Padel suggests that "level" refers to the flow of the water. It's certainly a watery place, with its stream running through a marshy valley, into which the water collecting underground at the nearby lead mines flows via at least one adit. Well up the valley a leat used to take water from the stream to power two waterwheels - one overshot and one undershot - at what was, at least until the start of this century, an imposing three-storey manorial corn mill, attached to the miller's cottage or cottages. (Apparently there were two dwellings originally.) "Fentengempes" or "Fentergempys" Mill is mentioned in documents as far back as 1330 and 1413. In later centuries it became known as "Shewsy's Mill". The present owner of the former mill barn beside the 17th-century bridge, now converted into an attractive house, told me the mill was sold, many years ago, to a scrap merchant who proceeded to gut it, not only of all the machinery but of every saleable item including the wooden beams - hence the sad condition it is now (November 1993) in, not only derelict but dangerously close to collapse. Perhaps it will have been swept away completely by the time you do this walk.

❶ After crossing the bridge at Ventongimps (*), continue up this country road for half a mile. A clear track on the edge of woodland meets the road here, going off both left and right. To visit the lead mine sites you could simply go on along the road, and continue following the directions from point 3; but for an attractive walk through open farmland, woods and the Chyverton House estate, take the left-hand track. After a few hundred yards, follow the prominent track among trees on the right. Ignore the right turning almost at the start of it. Soon the track bears right, into an open field, but you need to keep straight on. The path runs between two low walls, or "hedges". (In Cornwall the word "hedge" is often used to refer to dry-stone walling; such walls are filled with earth,

and after a short time the stone is usually almost hidden by plant growth, as well as providing homes for vast numbers of insects and other small animal life.) **After about 150 yards, the way ahead is blocked by shrubby growth, and here you bear right, keeping fairly near the hedge on your right at first. The path is not very clear, but if you stay in the woodland and keep going roughly straight ahead you will soon descend into a small valley - you may need to duck under a fallen tree unless it has been cleared by now - where there are two footbridges (granite and wood/earth) over a stream.** Take care not to slip if you use the granite one; the other is not slippery but may be rather more likely to collapse. What a choice! Country walking can be fraught with excitement.... After this adventure, **go up slightly to the right, where you need to step over a low barbed-wire fence.** (Some wood has been attached, presumably to make things easier, but I'm not convinced it succeeds. "Is this a walk or an assault course?" I hear you cry.) **Now walk across the open field (almost straight on - very slightly left) and through the gap at the corner of the hedge of the next field. From here to the road at Little Callestock the path is obvious, running on the left side of the hedge, though encroaching brambles here and there may force you to walk along the edge of the field above.**

❷ **At the road, turn right, and then bear right** on the pretty road, lined in spring with primroses, violets and bluebells, through the Chyverton estate, whose pheasants you may well hear if not see. Just before you reach a T-junction you will be able to see Chyverton House (*) on the left. **Turn left at the T-junction.**

CHYVERTON HOUSE

The name seems to mean "the house on the grassland"; Bill Trembath also mentions the possibilities of "the house upon the hill" and "the house by the spring". The original farmhouse, part of the huge Arundell estate, was replaced by the present mansion about 1781. For many years it belonged to the Thomas family, prominent in Cornish mining concerns, and they developed the large garden, landscaped in the Georgian manner with lake and bridge. In 1820 it was described as displaying "many beauties, consisting of neat sheets of water, fine gardens, and thriving plantations." In our century it has been further enhanced by a large collection of exotic shrubs and trees, the magnolias being particularly famous. Mr Trembath's book gives detailed information about the garden and its plants. From the beginning of March to the end of May, if you want to visit the garden you need to write to Mr and Mrs N. T. Holman, Chyverton, Zelah, Truro TR4 9DH, or telephone (0872-54324) for an appointment. Please try to give at least a week's notice.

West Chiverton stamps-engine house, from a photograph taken in 1937.
Little besides the boiler house now remains.

❸ **After a few yards, just before the main entrance to Chyverton, turn right on to a well-surfaced track. Soon this bends sharply right; follow it round, ignoring the left turning,** and you now come to the surviving buildings of the West Chiverton Lead Mine (*). When I originally researched this book the engine house was surrounded by huge burrows, but this is now designated a "land fill site", and the landscape is undergoing drastic transformation by the agency of lorries and earth-movers. The engine house can be approached by means of a track on the far side. In the winter of 1993-4 there were notices forbidding entry, but I can only presume that these refer to vehicles, since, unless I am totally misinterpreting my "Pathfinder" map, this is officially a "road used as a public path"; the kissing-gate beside the main gate would seem to confirm this. After inspecting the engine house, return through the gate to the main track. As you continue the walk you have a good view southwards, and can just make out among trees the ruined engine house of Chiverton Moor Mine, which the walk is now heading for. **The track curves left as it reaches the road.**

THE WEST CHIVERTON LEAD MINE

Apart from East Wheal Rose, this was Cornwall's most important lead mine, and it also produced nearly one and a quarter million ounces of silver. Its main period of activity was between 1859 and 1886, and the amount of waste material dumped shows how busy a mine it was; in 1870 it was employing 1,000 people. A large quantity of zinc was recovered from the dumps after the mining had ceased. The engine house at Batter's Shaft is particularly impressive, being three storeys high and built with unusual attention to detail. In 1869 an 80-inch pumping engine was installed here, made by Harvey & Co. of Hayle; it was reputed to be an exceptionally fine one. After the mine closed it was moved to United Mines at Gwennap, and later to Great Condurrow near Camborne. At both sites its house is still visible. The builders at West Chiverton made the task of installing and removing the huge engine harder by placing the stack at the centre of the

15

wall opposite the bob wall; nearly all other houses had a large opening at this point for that purpose: to use a side entrance was much more awkward. The unusual design was said to be to make the east wall of the house, with its huge "cylinder doorway" and arched windows, impressive when seen by visitors and shareholders of the mine calling at the count house. On the east side of the engine house - the side from which you approach - was the dam where the "tailings" (waste materials suspended in water) were put to settle out, and beyond that were the dressing floors and the stamps: the stamps engine house was eventually blown up (in 1952, and without warning, much to the disgust of all who valued Cornwall's mining heritage), but the boiler house and some fragments of the engine house remain.

❹ **Turn left on the road, and after about a quarter of a mile go through a five-bar wooden farm gate on the right, which comes about fifty yards before the hedge between two quite large fields.** (In case you are in doubt: the gate in question is set back a few feet from the road, and when we last did this walk was secured on the bottom-left corner with a short length of chain.) **Walk straight down the slope, parallel with the hedge to your left, and at the bottom, close to the corner of the field, cross the stone footbridge and go through the small wooden gate. Now go straight across the next field, heading for the ruined engine house. Go through the six-bar metal farm gate by a small stream. The path to follow now runs on the right side of the hedge in front of you;** in November 1993 access to this public footpath was blocked by means of a metal gate tied in position. This was easy enough to climb over, but had what looked like electric fencing wound through it. Once you have surmounted that barrier you will soon come to the remaining bob wall (i.e. the thickest wall of the engine-house, which supported the weight of the bob or beam of the pumping engine) of the Chiverton Moor Mine (*). The site is now badly overgrown, but the hollows and hillocks in quite an extensive area, mainly to the west, are obvious relics of its spoil-heaps.

THE CHIVERTON MOOR MINE

An ancient mine, known once as Great Callestock Moor, this was a much smaller enterprise than West Chiverton, producing about 2,240 tons of lead and 24,000 ounces of silver between 1847 and 1873. The engine house was built about 1863 for a 70-inch beam engine to pump the water from shafts which had reached 500 feet in depth by 1870. 150 people were employed here then.

Go on past the ruin for a few yards, and then bear right, along a few yards of rather overgrown path and through a five-bar wooden farm gate, not made any the easier to open by having only one hinge. Go diagonally across the small field to a gap on the right, which brings you into a bigger field. Walk by the hedge on your left for a few yards, and you will find a seven-bar metal gate with an old stone stile on its left. Cross this, and now you are on a lane leading direct to Callestick (*). (No problems with finding your way, but when I was last there the mud was well up to usual West Country standards, especially at the far end.)

❺ **At the road, in the attractive hamlet of Callestick, turn right, and then right again, signposted to Perran Church and Perranporth.**

CALLESTICK

Pronounced as three syllables with the stress on the second one, the name appears also as "Callestock", but Oliver Padel considers it unlikely to be the same in meaning as "Calstock", a name of English origin, as is true of many place-names in the easternmost part of the county. "Callestick" probably derives from the Cornish language, but its meaning is obscure. Bill Trembath writes of the days when Callestick was populated mainly by miners, and had its own pub, the Albert Inn, which closed in 1893 as a result of the decline of local mining. In 1826 the first Wesleyan chapel in the parish was built at Callestick.

Callestick Farm, on the corner, advertises Cornish dairy ice cream for sale. (To visit the Callestock Cider Farm, which is normally open from 9 a.m. to 6 p.m. every day except Sunday between March and Christmas, ignore for the moment the right turning to Perran Church; follow the road round past the telephone box. Go straight on up the hill, past the farm house and a chapel. The Cider Farm is signposted on the left.) If your car is parked at the White House Inn, you could continue along the road signposted to Perran Church, going straight on at the crossroads; you will reach the

A3075 just a few yards from the Inn. **To return to Ventongimps, take the first right turning**, a narrow, pretty road - little more than a lane, and well laced with mud - which passes Venton Vaise ("spring in the open field") farm. **Turn right again at the "main" road, which leads into Ventongimps.**

On the right before the bridge you will see a notice mentioning that there is a reserve here, belonging to the Cornwall Trust for Nature Conservation. The reserve is open to the public, but waterproof footwear is essential - or bare feet! There are about twenty acres of wet heath, bog and damp woodland, and a pond formed in 1970 when the remains of a crashed World War II bomber were dug out. Many types of butterfly thrive here, including the Marsh Fritillary, which was re-introduced at Ventongimps after becoming rare in the West Country. It also seems likely that snipe and quail are breeding in the reserve; but the main interest is to botanists, since the mosaic of wet and dry areas has encouraged unusual plants such as the Dorset Heath to flourish. More information can be obtained from the CTNC at Five Acres, Allet, Truro (0872-73939), or from the Warden, Mrs Jane King, 1 Rosemundy, St Agnes (0872-553441).

West Chiverton Mine, 1989: remains of the boiler house for the stamps engine. Pumping-engine house on Batter's Shaft in the distance.

WALK 3
BOLINGEY, NEW CHIVERTON, WHEAL ALBERT AND ST PIRAN'S ROUND

About 7 miles - slightly shorter if Wheal Albert is omitted

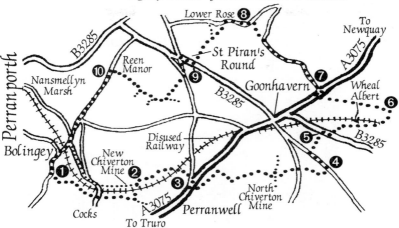

Directions are also given for a 2-mile walk based on Bolingey.

Bolingey, a very pretty old village, has a general store and a nice, cosy pub, the Bolingey Inn. (I recommend their oxtail soup - a meal in itself!) The first half of the route runs alongside a disused railway. If you do the full walk you will see the remains of several mines, two of which still have engine houses, although both are in an advanced state of decay. Near the end of the walk is an impressive, well-preserved ancient fort and "playing place". Most of the route is on well-made tracks; one part, around Wheal Albert, is marshy, and you can omit this section if you prefer. If you were to attempt the Wheal Albert part of the walk in winter or during a wet spell you would almost certainly need wellington boots. Near the half-way point on the walk, you could, during the season, visit "The World in Miniature", which features accurate models of famous buildings, statues and other marvels from all over the world. There is a cafeteria on the site. For those who want only a short, easy walk, a two-mile version is suggested, visiting Bolingey and New Chiverton mine only.

To drive to Bolingey from St Agnes, take the B3285 east to Perranporth, and from there go south on the B3284. After about a mile, Bolingey is signposted to the left. In the village, turn right at the T-junction, passing the Bolingey Inn, and you should find room to park on the left just before Bolingey Lake. From Truro, take the A390 westwards to the Chiverton Cross roundabout, then the A3075 towards Newquay, and then turn left on to the B3284 to Perranporth. About a mile before Perranporth, turn right where signposted to Bolingey; from there, follow the directions above.

WALK 3

BOLINGEY

The name means "mill house" and appears elsewhere in Cornwall in such forms as "Mellingey", "Melinsey" and possibly also "Valency". (The stream that flows past the New Chiverton engine house is called the Mellingey or Molingy, and there is a Mellingey Cottage a mile or so up-stream in Penwartha Coombe: see Walk 4.) A photograph showing the two overshot waterwheels at Bolingey Mill (on the route of this walk, near the end) is in D.E.Benney's "Cornish Watermills", and it is presumably the same mill that is depicted on the inn sign in the village.

A cottage in Bolingey

❶ **Continue in the direction you were driving for a few yards, and then turn left over a bridge. At the houses the track bears left,** near the lake, and takes you through an attractive little valley dominated by a hill which was ablaze with gorse in March. **You cross a tiny stream; at the road, with the hamlet of Cocks on the right, continue on the public footpath opposite. Go over the stone stile on the left side of a gate**, and soon you see an engine house on the other side of the valley: this is at New Engine Shaft of New Chiverton Mine (*).

NEW CHIVERTON MINE

This mine, otherwise known as Old Wheal Anne, had a 40-inch pumping engine in 1864 and was mining to a depth of over 300 feet. In 1870 it was employing 50 people. Between 1864 and its closure in 1878 it produced 300 tons of lead, 640 tons of zinc, a little iron and arsenic, and 1,300 ounces of silver. Many local people know New Chiverton as Calley Mine - or perhaps that name is more accurately applied only to the section at New Engine Shaft. An article by Alice M. Bizley in "Old Cornwall" (Autumn 1983) refers to an old man whose father could remember when the boiler was taken out at Calley: a team of 22 horses was required to draw it away. The ghosts that are supposed to haunt the mine at night may, Mrs Bizley suggests, be the barn owls that live in the engine house.

After passing through the gate, you soon reach another gate with a high stile on its left; ignore this and go over the smaller stile a few yards further left. You cross a small stream by stepping stones and a larger one by a bridge, then go under the viaduct which once carried the loop line from Chacewater to Newquay via Mount Hawke, St Agnes, Goonbell, Mithian, Perranporth, Goonhavern, the Lappa Valley and Trewerry & Trerice (see Walks 1 and 10 and "Around Newquay" for details), **over another small bridge, and after a few steps down a wall the path runs uphill to meet a wider track.**

❷ Here you could turn left to have a closer look at the engine house; the path passes about twenty feet below it. A photograph of this engine house as it was in 1935 is in H.G.Ordish's 1967 volume. The house close by was originally the mine's count house, and there are also the ruinous remains of what may have been the miners' dry.

For the short walk, continue ahead down the valley, and at the road still go on in the same direction. Keep to the lower road, ignoring the right fork, and after about another quarter of a mile you will reach a crossroads; Mill Road, on the left, will take you back into Bolingey, as described near the start of point 10.

To continue the full walk, return along the same path and keep straight on, crossing a stile on the right of a gate. On your right are the stream and a pond. Bear right to pass under a railway bridge.

❸ At the road - a very busy one, so take care - cross, go a few yards to the right, and then take the track going sharp left. (But first you might be interested to walk up to the converted Perranwell chapel buildings, dating from 1843 and 1867, rather stranded now at a higher level than the main road. The white wooden building next to them, now in use as a bric-a-brac shop, is a surprising survival from the old Nobel Dynamite Works at Cligga Head (Walk 7), purchased in 1918 for £200 as a Sunday School building.) **After the houses, continue ahead along a narrow, often muddy path. When this meets a wider track, ignore the track going left: continue ahead, keeping to the main track as it bears right. Fork left before a metal gate, the entrance to Pensilva Farm. After quite a long, straight, uphill stretch, part of which runs beside the land belonging to the Silverbow Park camping and caravan site, the track curves right and left;** there is a small patch of woodland on the left, where the ground seems to have been disturbed by mining, and on the right is a capped shaft. This was North Chiverton mine (*), and soon you are surrounded by waste tips and capped shafts.

WALK 3

NORTH CHIVERTON MINE

This was opened in 1863, re-working an older mine called Wheal Anna, dating from at least 1836. An illustration of the immense efforts and determination which went into Cornish mining is that to drain these workings a deep adit nearly 5,000 feet long had been dug, starting in the valley near Perranwell. In 1863 a house was built to take a 50-inch engine; by 1867 the main shaft was down to about 700 feet, and 44 people were employed at the mine; but the lode did not fulfil expectations, and work ceased the following year. The sales recorded for those five years were 100 tons of lead ore, 630 tons of blende (zinc sulphide), a little iron and 3,640 ounces of silver.

Next, ignore the tracks to right and left: take the one that bears slightly right, then left past a pair of cottages converted into one house. You now join a narrow path, cobbled at first but rather muddy later. Before long, this brings you to a road; cross that and continue on the track opposite.
(Alternatively, to shorten the walk somewhat and avoid a very wet section, leaving out the visit to Wheal Albert, you could turn left at the road and continue into Goonhavern; in the village either turn right on to the Newquay road, A3075, for about a mile and turn left, picking up the directions at point 7, or shorten the walk still more by going straight on towards Perranporth on the B3285 for about two miles, joining the main walk route again at St Piran's Round, point 9 in the directions. As you can see, both of these possibilities involve a good deal of walking on busy roads: I hope you will prefer to give the Wheal Albert route a try!)
This track passes to the left of a house (Higher Polgoda Farm) via two gates, becomes a grassy path and later joins a wider track.

❹ **Turn left at the road, and just past the house on the left ("Accra"), take the track on the right, passing the entrance to the Greenmeadows Caravan Park.**

❺ **At the next road, turn right, by the entrance to "The World in Miniature", and take the first track on the left, by a house called "Tremorna"** (unless by now it has changed). **After the houses** (the last of which is named "Count House", and therefore seems likely to have belonged to the mine that lies ahead), **go straight on, over a wooden stile on the right side of a rickety, rusty and bent gate.** Now the path is very boggy, but passable if you choose your route with care. On the left here, close to the course of the disused railway line, is a small reserve called Carn Moor, cared for by the Cornwall Trust for Nature Conservation; like the Ventongimps reserve nearby (Walk 2) this is a wetland area (you hardly needed to be told!) where snipe, herons and buzzards may be seen. Soon you reach the ruinous and overgrown engine house of Wheal Albert (*), where the path was soggiest of all late in 1993 when I last did this walk.

WALK 3

WHEAL ALBERT

This was first worked in 1826 under the name of Goonhavern Mine. Renamed Wheal Albert in the 1850s - perhaps as a tribute to royalty, like Prince Royal Mine in Perrancoombe - it was worked with the aid of a larger (24-inch) engine, and in the 1860s a 45-inch engine was installed. The ruined engine house is the one built for that. Hamilton Jenkin says the mine closed in 1867, but according to J.H.Collins it was employing 70 people in 1870. The metals recovered were mainly lead and zinc.

Wheal Albert,
from a 1935 photograph

After this, go through a wooden five-bar gate, past a small corrugated-iron cowshed, then left, through a second similar gate with a yellow waymark arrow attached. At about this point you are crossing the old railway track. A third gate of the same type bears a white arrow pointing right; following that brings you to a small stile - a short length of wooden fencing to enable you to cross a barbed wire fence. Follow the obvious path ahead between gorse patches and soon you will see a wooden stile. "Path around Pond" says a notice on the stile: a few steps ahead bring you to the pond, after which walk a few more yards beside the little stream and cross a low, mossy wall with the aid of a few steps. Now walk left - rather wet and a little overgrown here - to another stile.

❻ Turn left on the wide track, passing quite close to Wheal Albert engine house again. This track continues for nearly a mile. At the road turn right, again taking great care.

❼ Next turn left on to a quiet, attractive little road, passing the Newperran Tourist Park and later Paradise Cottage. The farm soon after this is called Wheal Hope, and if you look down to the left you will see signs of old mining activity. This was a small lead mine; apparently the hope was not fulfilled, because no record remains of its output. Not far past the farm, the road curves right; go down the track on the left here. Where the track bends sharp left, go straight on, and at the next left bend go ahead on to the narrow grassy path which brings you down to the road.

❽ **Turn left, crossing the stream by the bridge beside the ford** (although a culvert takes the stream underneath the road, so the bridge is needed only in very wet spells). Mr Roger Glanville tells me that this place, locally known as "Tommascotty", was another one where water-powered Cornish stamps (for crushing tin ore) once operated: compare the comments on Stampas Farm in Walk 5. **Then continue up the road till you reach the houses and cottages of Lower Rose (*).**

ROSE

To trot out the oft-repeated remark about the Roseland, this name has nothing to do with flowers, but probably derives from the Cornish "ros", moorland. The interesting article about Rose in the WI's "Cornwall Village Book", however, mentions two rival explanations. One relates to the local belief that the original settlement was closer to the sea and was engulfed by the ever-shifting sands, like St Piran's Oratory and the mythical city of Langona or Langarrow. (See the note on Cubert Common in "Around Newquay".) The story goes that the surviving villagers moved inland and built a new village, calling it "Rose" because it rose from the sand. The other explanation is that the name derives from a Celtic word meaning circle or wheel, referring to St Piran's Round. The same article describes Rose when the local mines were active: "it had four shops, two pubs, a bakery and a shoemaker, and a population of about 1,400." The disappearance of shops (apart from the little post office, which currently opens only twice a week) is in fact a much more recent event than the demise of the mines: people living there now tell me it's not long since there were three.

Opposite the lane on the right to Lowertown Farm Barn there is a field gate on the left. Go through that and walk along the path ahead, on the left edge of the field. Go through the second gate on the left, bear right and then go straight on through a gate to join a lane. This is locally called "Stile Lane": the story goes that at the Lower Rose end of it there were originally steps to help the bearers at walking funerals going to the old parish church in the sands. **Just as you reach the road, go through the gate on your right to visit St Piran's Round (*).**

ST PIRAN'S ROUND

Otherwise known as Piran Round or Perran Round, this was first recorded in 1747 (Martyn's map), but it almost certainly originated as a fortified settlement surrounded by a circular bank of earth and stone which gave protection from the weather and wild animals such as wolves, as well as human enemies. It has been suggested that in Cornwall as many as a thousand such sites were constructed and occupied around the time of the Roman occupation of Britain. In about the 14th and 15th centuries this particular "round" was adapted as one of many medieval amphitheatres in Cornwall where the miracle plays were performed. (Elsewhere they are usually called "Plain an Gwarry" or "Playing Place". The only other one which is anything like as well preserved as this is in the centre of St Just-in-Penwith: see "A View from Carn Galver", Walk 2.) It appears that at Piran Round a second entrance was made, opposite the original one, and steps were cut in the bank to make seats for the audience. Hamilton Jenkin ("Cornwall and its People") writes: "In the bottom .... may still be seen a three-foot pit which perhaps served as the infernal region...." (The pit Jenkin mentions is known locally as the Devil's Frying Pan. Tradition says if you run round it seven times and then put your ear to the ground in the middle you can hear the devil frying souls. In addition to, or instead of, representing Hell, it may have been used to create the illusion of people or animals rising from the ground, as for example in the Creation scenes.) "During the performance," he continues," the position of the actors in the 'plain' itself was carefully orientated. God and Heaven took the east; the Devil and Hell the north; worldly potentates were assigned to the west; whilst saints and good characters occupied the south. 'Distinguished characters,' writes Mr Nance, 'had their own "tents", "palaces" or "towers", probably consisting at the most, of sentry-boxes made of wood.' In some cases Heaven appears to have been represented by a scaffold erected above the plain. In 1575 an entry in the borough accounts of St Ives records: 'Spent upon the carpenters that made hevin, 4d'." Between 1969 and 1973 several performances of the Cornish play-cycle, the Ordinalia, were given at Piran Round; these plays seem to have been written between 1350 and 1500 at Glasney College, Penryn. Betty Roberts, the Administrator at Piran Round when it was reopened, wrote in the 1973 programme about the drawbacks and advantages of performing in the open air. "St Piran was in the middle of his big speech. 'Give me a sign Oh Lord,' he thundered. 'Give me a sign.' The Lord, very obligingly, I felt, decided to co-operate, and, right on cue, sent a flash of lightning and a roll of thunder."

❾ Turn right on the road - another busy one, I'm afraid, but you soon leave it, following the sign to Reen Cross and Perranwell on the left. Before the houses, take the track on the right, where from the gaps in the hedge you have wide, open views. On the skyline ahead is Mithian Church, close to the big Chiverton roundabout on the A30; Perranporth, too, is ahead, but hidden in its valley, and further right is St Agnes Beacon. The wind farm at Carland Cross can be seen by looking back when you have gone a few hundred yards along the track. This is "Jack's Lane", called after Jacka's Shaft, which was in a field on the right. The shafts of Budnick Mine, of which this was one, were named after mining families from Rose, including Hooper and Bice. Budnick was at its most prosperous in the first half of last century but continued in production till 1904, and the area was prospected again between the wars. Copper, tin, lead, silver and zinc were all produced at various periods. **At the T-junction turn right; ignore the left fork soon after, and carry on past Higher Reen Farm (notice the fine view of Perranporth from here) to join the road at Reen Manor.** The lane you joined at the T-junction was once the road from Perranporth to Goonhavern, travelled on foot daily by many schoolchildren at a time when the only school in Perranporth was for infants. Other children went to school in Penwartha Coombe: see Walk 4.

Trees in Pencrennow Lane, near Reen Manor

⓿ Turn left, and now continue along this pretty little road, with some spectacularly bent trees and bushes - a result of salt-laden winds which stunt growth on the windward side - and a good view over Perranporth to the sea, **for about a mile. Ignore the left turn and descend into the valley. Cross the main road** (but see the note about Nansmellyn Marsh) **and keep straight on along Mill Road into Bolingey.** You cross the mill leat almost at once. The corn mill, now converted into an attractive house, is on the left; its two waterwheels were roughly where the flight of stairs now is. **After the shop, cross two bridges over streams separated by the old railway bridge. Walk on up Penwartha Road and past the Bolingey Inn to return to your car.**

NANSMELLYN MARSH

There is a nature reserve in the care of the Cornwall Trust for Nature Conservation at Nansmellyn ("Mill Valley") Marsh, which you could visit by turning right instead of going along Mill Road into Bolingey. After about a quarter of a mile, take the path on the right at Nansmellyn Farm. The reserve consists of ten or eleven acres covered mostly by willows and reed-beds, and is remarkable as a breeding ground for 58 species of birds and 90 species of butterflies and moths. The river there is full of trout. There is a bird hide on the eastern side, and early in 1994 a new boardwalk leading to that has been constructed with the aid of a grant from Marks & Spencer and the Civic Trust. Visitors who respect the flora and fauna are welcome, but must stay on the paths and keep dogs on leads. Further details can be obtained from the CTNC at 5 Acres, Allet, Truro (Telephone: Truro 73939).

WALK 4

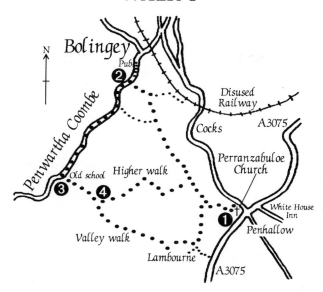

PERRANZABULOE CHURCH, BOLINGEY AND PENWARTHA COOMBE

About 3 miles

This is a charming walk, and amazingly varied for so short a route. The main points of interest, apart from the scenery and long views, are the church - less than two centuries old, but much of it salvaged from its medieval predecessor - and the use of water-power in the valley. Mining has also had its effect on this landscape, though this fact is less obvious today than on the other walks in this book. Pleasant pubs offering good food are conveniently situated at the start-end point (the White House Inn, Penhallow) and half-way (the Bolingey Inn). Bolingey also has a general store. The going is easy throughout, but you have to be prepared to climb or scramble around one or two gates, and waterproof footwear would be essential except in unusually dry spells.

The suggested start-and-end point is Perranzabuloe Parish Church (*). Directions for driving there from St Agnes or Truro are given at the start of Walk 2. Immediately beyond the church turn left (i.e. north-west, towards Perranporth). There is usually room to park in the layby on the left, but please avoid doing so at times of church services, when you should still be able to park on the left side of the road a little further along.

WALK 4

PERRANZABULOE PARISH CHURCH

The history of this building is a sequel to the events described in the note on St Piran's Oratory, Cross and Church in Walk 5. As said there, the building of the new church began in 1804; it was consecrated in July 1805. If it looks rather older than that, this is because much of the tower, some window tracery and several inside features were salvaged from the Norman church. Parts of the lychgate, too, were rescued from the church in the sands. Since most of the population of Perranzabuloe parish lives two miles away at Perranporth, a chapel of ease (St Michael's) was built there in 1872.

❶ **Enter the churchyard by the gate beside the layby and go round the far side of the church to the main entrance, the south door.** Notice, close to that, the ancient, small Cornish cross salvaged from St Piran's Oratory before that was reburied under the sands in 1980. (There is a note about the Oratory in Walk 5.) **To start the walk, take the path leading from the south door,** past a seat and the attractive Trembath Garden, where rosebeds surround a collection of small memorial tablets. **The path continues to the right, downhill, beside a Cornish hedge on your left. After a few steps down, it continues for a while between hedges to a low stone stile, where you join a wider track. Continue in the same direction, and where the track ends at an open field still keep straight on towards the sea, heading slightly left of Perranporth to a gap in the hedge.** On the skyline to your right are the windmills at Carland Cross; also to the right but much closer is the quite deep valley in which used to run the branch line from Chacewater to Newquay (details in Walks 1, 3 & 9), and as you continue downhill you will see the engine house of New Chiverton

Mine, also visited on Walk 3. **On the other side of the gap in the hedge there is a short length of wooden fencing to enable you to cross a barbed-wire fence, though not everyone will find it easy to negotiate. Now keep by the fence on your right, cross the stile at the field corner (to the right of a double farm-gate) and continue down to the next corner. Here you will probably have to climb the gate, because when we did this walk it had become too overgrown at the hinge end to be moved. After that, walk to the left of the bungalow, and at the wide track go left, soon crossing the bridge over the Penwartha stream.**

❷ At the road, turn right past the entrance to the Bolingey Lake angling club if you want to visit Bolingey, possibly to get refreshments at the pub or shop. The Bolingey Inn (on which I have commented in the note at the start of Walk 3) is only a few hundred yards along the road, but for the shop you need to continue beyond the railway bridge. (By the way, you may, like us, be intrigued by the tall chimney stack rising from a bank near houses behind the pub. It is, we were told, just a domestic chimney, originally belonging to a small hotel, and may have been made so tall in order to reduce the risk of setting fire to the thatched roofs that were close by when it was built.) Return the same way and go on ahead up the valley road to continue the walk.

If you don't want to go to Bolingey now, turn left on reaching the road. Now comes a delightful walk up Penwartha Coombe. ("Penwartha", often spelt "Penwortha" on older maps and documents, presumably means "head of the summit" or "upper head", which seems very odd for this place; but Penwortha Farm, from which the valley takes its name, stands on higher ground.) I guess the road sometimes carries a fair amount of traffic in summer, but in January 1994 when we last walked along it all was quiet apart from the roaring stream, whose water was remarkably clear despite the torrential rains which had so recently devastated parts of Cornwall, notably Polperro: one might have expected the run-off from fields to have made the water pretty turbid here, too. (Don't be deceived by the clarity into drinking it, however: warning signs further up the valley insist it is polluted.) The power in a stream like this would have been put to good use in former times. As I have mentioned elsewhere, the name "Bolingey" indicates that there was a watermill there; and soon you will reach another former mill, Nanslone. ("Nans" means valley; "lone" may perhaps derive from a Celtic word meaning "grove, thicket".) The waterwheel, made at the Redruth Foundry in 1906, is still in place, and the course of the millstream which supplied it is still obvious a few feet above the road on the right side further up the valley. Evidently the water was fed by a concrete launder to a pipe which carried it under the road, suggesting that the wheel was undershot, but this is not necessarily so. Bill Trembath states that the mill was probably for "tucking" or fulling cloth. Not far beyond the mill there is a steep path up on the right; this may well have been created originally in connection with one of the small mines in this valley (*). Soon after the road crosses the stream, notice the mouth of what I take to be a mine adit behind the low bank on the left side of the road; the lower part of it is now choked.

The wheel at Nanslone Mill

MINES IN AND NEAR PENWARTHA COOMBE

There were at least four: Perran Wheal Jane, otherwise called Penwortha Consols; South Wheal Leisure, otherwise Truro Consols; West Shepherds; and Lambriggan. These mines, active mainly in the mid-19th century, produced principally copper, plus a certain amount of tin, iron, silver, lead and zinc. A.K.H. Jenkin gives many colourful details about some of these mines, including an account of the slap-up dinner at Pearce's Hotel, St Agnes, that was arranged to celebrate the start of Perran Wheal Jane in 1852. "Throughout the day," he writes, "the bells rang merry peals and the evening was enlivened by performances of the St Agnes amateur brass band. Apparently the cost of these festivities proved too much for the finances of the company whose activities terminated shortly afterwards."

Continue past the Old School House, and the former school itself, dating from 1878. In its early years children from all over the parish came here: Perranporth had no school till 1898. Bill Trembath gives interesting and amusing details about the school's first headmaster and what it was like to be a pupil here.

❸ **Turn left immediately past the school, following the sign Public Byway.** (But notice, as you do so, that the cottage almost opposite is called Mellingey, which like Bolingey means "mill-house". The present owner told us that the mill itself, a corn mill, was at the further end of the building, close to the bank which carried the leat, and the end nearer the road was the miller's cottage.) The byway runs beside a tributary stream in another pretty valley.

❹ **When you come to a footbridge you have a choice of ways,** both attractive but extremely different.

A valley walk (WARNING: This route is likely to be practicable only in unusually dry weather or for those well kitted-out with wellies. After the rains of late 1993 / early 1994 we gave up the attempt to get through, although in fact the flood-barrier that stopped us was probably less than 100 yards long even then. Another deterrent on this path is that a few gates have to be climbed or scrambled around. Despite all this, and the mud churned up by cattle, it's worth a try because it's such a pretty walk, mostly among trees beside the stream, even if you do find you have to turn back.) **For this route, cross the stile a few feet to the left of the gate and walk beside the stream on your right - or as close to it as the mud allows.** It was just beyond the third gate that we found our way barred by a mini-lake. If you succeed in getting past that, **keep to the track as it goes uphill between hedges. Soon you join a wider track and pass between a bungalow and some farm buildings. At the T-junction, where you have Lambourne Manor on your right, turn left and continue along this track till it bends left.** (Lambourne was an important manor in medieval times, and the site of a chapel of St Edmund, but by the time Thomas Tonkin described it - about 1736 - the mansion had fallen into decay, its stones had been taken for other houses, and the chapel converted to a dwelling.) **There cross the low stone stile on your right, and you will soon be back at the church.**

A walk on high ground (This one was problem-free when we tried it; not pretty but offering panoramic views on a clear day.) **For this, turn left, following the signpost to the church. After the stony, uphill track, cross a high concrete stile beside a metal gate and then keep to the right side of the field, crossing another similar stile and then a lower granite one.** At this point the view includes the Carland Cross windfarm, the spoil heaps of china-clay country, and the sea above Perranporth; looking behind, you can see St Agnes Beacon and the lonely Mithian Church on the skyline. **Now turn right, still keeping to the hedge on your right, and over another granite stile. Not far past that you rejoin the path you used at the start: turn right, and continue ahead at the low stile to return to the church.**

WALK 5

HOLYWELL, ELLENGLAZE, ST PIRAN'S ORATORY AND PENHALE PT
with an optional extension to
CUBERT

About 8 miles (nearly 9 with Cubert)

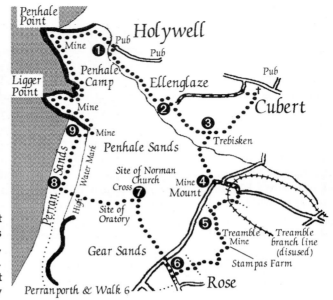

This is the longest and most arduous walk in the book, but a very fine one. It is full of interest for the local history enthusiast and the industrial archaeologist; the big army camp at Penhale may just be a blot on the landscape for some, but for others it will add further interest. The views from Ligger and Penhale Points extend almost forty miles along the coast. The scenery is splendid and varied, including some truly awe-inspiring clifftop walking and a gentle inland section beside streams and through undulating farmland. Separating the cliffs and the farms is the strange, empty world of dunes called Gear Sands, hidden in which are the sites of an ancient oratory and a medieval church. There are toilets and a choice of pubs and shops at Holywell, but no other source of refreshments unless you are prepared to make the short diversion into Cubert, adding a little over half a mile to the walk. There are public toilets there, as well as shops and a pub.
WARNING: The coastal path around Ligger and Penhale headlands runs close to the edge in places, and might be best avoided in rough weather and by those who suffer from vertigo.
(If you want a longer walk, linking this route to the next one but omitting the section including the Oratory, see the note at the end of Walk 6.)

To drive to Holywell (*), take the A390 west from Truro or the B3277 south-east from St Agnes, and turn on to the A3075 Newquay road at Three Burrows (Chiverton roundabout). From Perranporth take the B3285 to Goonhavern and turn left on the main road there. Holywell is signposted on the left about three miles beyond Goonhavern. There are two quite large car parks at Holywell (one of them free to National Trust members), but both may be full at peak holiday times.

WALK 5

HOLYWELL

There may have been a Celtic saint called Cubert, or something similar: Catherine Rachel John believes the name is a corruption of "Gwbert", who hailed from the Cardigan area. Another theory is that the saint associated with Cubert village and Holywell is Cuthbert of Lindisfarne in Northumberland, which of all places in England is about the furthest away. The story, or legend, is that about a century after his death in 687, the monks of Lindisfarne had to flee because of Viking raids. They sailed for Ireland, taking with them the remains of St Cuthbert, but storms drove them ashore just south of Kelsey Head, where there was already a holy well. St Cuthbert's "reliques accidentally touched the well and to it communicated their qualities." Later the monks were told in a dream to return northwards; they travelled overland to Durham and laid the Saint's remains to rest in the cathedral. (Oliver Padel in "Cornish Place-Names" appears to support the case for St Cuthbert, saying that he is honoured at Gwbert in Cardiganshire too.) No-one knows for sure which of the two "holy wells" nearby is THE holy well. The O.S. "Pathfinder" map marks the one on the beach simply as "Cave", whereas the inland well, north of Trevornick, is labelled "Holy Well (restored)" (the restoration was carried out by Newquay Old Cornwall Society). This one is on land owned by the Trevornick Holiday Park. The one on the beach is in a smallish cave on the north side, close to low-water mark; for fuller directions and a description, see "Around Newquay", page 66 in the second edition. As for Holywell itself, the trade in holidays and retirement homes has made something of a shanty-town of it, and the dominant presence of the army, based at Penhale Camp, hardly improves matters. There are compensations, though: the old, or at least "olde worlde", Treguth Inn; the strangely beautiful, ever-shifting sandhills; the splendid beach; the magnificent cliff scenery both north and south; and the fascinating evidence of mining activity around Penhale and Ligger headlands.

❶ The walk starts on the path almost opposite the St Piran's Inn; if you are coming from the NT car park it is on the right just after you have crossed the bridge beside the pub. Ignore the track on the right at the sign, "The Meadow". After passing through (or beside) the Holywell Bay Holiday Park, follow the public footpath sign to Cubert and Ellenglaze, soon afterwards passing through a kissing-gate. The path runs beside the Holywell stream at first, through an area that is quite marshy in places - hence, perhaps, the name of the nearby headland, Penhale (Cornish, "head of the marsh"). This route was the official coastal footpath until the military authorities gave permission for it to skirt Penhale Camp on the seaward side; elderly acorn-signs still survive here and there. The next group of houses include Ellenglaze (*) Manor and Farm, and the path curves left to pass among them.

WALK 5

ELLENGLAZE

Ellenglaze Manor formerly comprised the whole of Cubert parish. It is mentioned in the Domesday Book, where it is called "Elil". Henderson states that "glaze", meaning "green", was added to distinguish it from the nearby manor of Elil-wyn (Helwyn or Halwyn), "the white Elil". This is mentioned again near the end of point 6 in the directions. According to a Carrick Official Guide, there is "a water wheel still in-situ behind the Manor House." A small lead-and-silver mine sank two shafts just north of Ellenglaze early in the 19th century, and its adit emptied into the marshy ground by Ellenglaze Farm - exactly where I do not know, but the disturbed area on the right of the path looks quite likely.

❷ **Where the track turns left and becomes Ellenglaze Lane, you have a choice of ways:**

A **Continue along Ellenglaze Lane in order to visit Cubert (*).** This quiet little road runs gently uphill for about half a mile. For the quickest route to Cubert church, **turn right at Churchfield Road, then left along a path which leads straight to the church via a kissing gate at the edge of the churchyard.** The shops are visible from the main (north) entrance to the churchyard. For the pub, a converted bungalow called the Tree Tops Inn, turn right at the main road, then left at the road to Crantock, just beyond the Cubert Garage.

Cubert Church

WALK 5

CUBERT

The original Cornish name for this village seems to have been something like Lanowyn or Lanlovey: Lanlovey Farm is nearby, and the first syllable means "church-site". (Henderson suggests that "Lanowyn" may allude to a saint called Noan, to whom three Breton churches are dedicated: Lannounan, Lannoan and Lanoan.) The later dedication of the church to "Sanctus Cubertus" (1269) or "Sanctus Cuthbertus" (1305) is discussed in the note about Holywell. Cubert's spire dates from the 14th century. Spires are not very common in Cornwall, and I suspect this one may have been added to make the tower even more prominent a landmark to guide sailors (compare St Keverne) - and perhaps also people trying to find their way across what Polsue (1867) calls the "deserts" of Cubert Common, the Kelseys, Penhale Sands and Gear Sands. Spire and church were devastated by lightning in April 1848 but restored, "sensitively", as John Betjeman puts it, by G.E.Street in 1852. Betjeman's verdict on the church, evidently one of his favourites, is "friendly, textured, holy and humble;" reading that prompts me to compare it with Sir John's "own" Cornish church of St Enodoc, another little spired church in a region dominated by dunes. One of the oldest parts of Cubert church is a Saxon memorial stone, built into the west wall of the tower. It reads "Conetoci fili Tejernomali", translated by Arthur Mee as "Conetocius, son of Tegerno, a sad loss"; Henderson, however, takes the last word to be "Tigernomaglus". Inside the church is a 13th-century font; the old benches have gone, but some of the bench-ends were used to make the pulpit, and the chancel roof still has much of its old carved timber. Both Tonkin (c.1736) and Polsue stress how "healthful" Cubert is, perhaps to reassure anyone who had heard of the "great plague" here in 1569, "by which died, from the 20th August to the 10th November, seventy people, and it then abating, from the 25th of December to the 23rd of February fifteen more" (Tonkin).

To resume the walk, leave the churchyard by the same kissing gate, then turn left immediately. Cross the estate road ahead and take the path almost opposite (very slightly to the right), which runs between bungalows. At the T-junction turn right, cross the stile and make for the right-hand edge of the field. (The right-of-way appears to cross the field diagonally, but if it is planted you may have to keep to the edge.) **The path runs downhill beside the hedge and through a kissing gate, after which there are hedges on both sides. After another stile, at the bottom turn right among the buildings of Trebisken** ("farmstead of the little copse or thicket", perhaps), **and then left at the coast path sign. Now pick up the directions near the start of point 3.**

B For the more direct route, turn right at the public footpath sign (to Trebisken). (There is a wooden gate at this point, and a sign for The Full

Bag Fly Fishery.) On the skyline to the right you can now see the stack of Mount Mine: see the later note on the Great Perran Iron Lode. **After passing the house, go diagonally to the right across the centre of the field, heading just to the left of the stack, and cross the stile at the field corner, which has an old coast path sign beside it. Next, go straight ahead to a gate, and through that on to a path running between two "hedges"** (earth-filled stone walls which in a very short time become smothered with vegetation).

❸ **Just after crossing a tiny stream - which may well disappear in a better-than-average summer - and before you reach a group of buildings (Trebisken), don't miss the right turning: there is a coast path sign, but it can easily be overlooked. You pass through a gate and then walk under windswept trees beside a hedge.** The footbridge is constructed partly of stout timbers which must surely once have been sleepers on the Treamble branch line. (There are notes on this - part of the Chacewater to Newquay loop - in Walks 1, 3 and 9. "Treamble" is said locally as "Tramble". The name was first recorded in 1316 as "Taranbol", "Thunderpool".) Around here the ground is marshy, but walking has been assisted by the use of more such sleepers. A little way to the left, just on the far side of the stream, are the remains of Trebisken and Trebellan Mines (*).

TREBISKEN AND TREBELLAN MINES

These small mines produced lead and also yielded silver. Records of mining here go back to Tudor times, when a German entrepreneur called Bernard Cranach or Burchard Kranich worked a mine at "Treworthie" (Treworthen Farm is on the route of this walk) and another at Legossick in St Issey parish, between Padstow and Wadebridge. He set up a smelting house for the silver at, of all unlikely places, Lerryn, near Lostwithiel. (See "Around the River Fowey", page 23.) After two hundred years of neglect, the mines appear to have been re-started about 1786, and about ten years later were optimistically named "Wheal Mexico". The finds of silver never quite lived up to that, although Hamilton Jenkin notes that "two small parcels of the richest silver-lead ore ever raised in Cornwall" were sold by the mine in 1860. By that time the operation was working under the name Cubert United. All mining appears to have ceased in 1864.

Cross the elaborate and gradually disintegrating wooden stile, and then head just to the left of the group of dark pines on the far side of what looks like an ancient golf-course. The path wanders a bit but is fairly clear. Cattle and farm vehicles have created something of a morass, I'm afraid, just before the gate.

❹ **Turn left at the road. Ignore the left turning after this; continue ahead, signposted to Rejerrah.** After crossing the stream, the road passes between the piers of a former bridge carrying the Treamble line. **At Treworthen farm, carry straight on along the track to the right of the farmhouse. At the next farm, North Treamble, turn right:** a pretty path through an area where both mining and quarrying took place. There are the remains of small burrows (spoil heaps) from Treamble iron mine close to the path, on the right as you go downhill (just before a more enclosed and level section which is usually muddy underfoot). Just before you reach the stream, notice the very substantial wooden gate-posts, one on either side if the path. These mark the point where the Treamble branch line crossed. The quarry was down by the stream: a small part of it is visible behind the modern pumping-station building, but the main pit, now flooded, lies beside the narrow path that cuts back sharply to the right just after you have crossed the bridge. Unfortunately the vegetation is usually too thick, especially in summer, for you to be able to see much. The quarry, which Roger Glanville believes worked until the early years of this century, was called Crows-an-Carn, meaning something like "the cross at the rock pile"; neither the cross nor the carn is evident now, so perhaps it's not surprising that the name got corrupted to "Cows and Corn", which was the name of a nearby field even when the quarry was still active. ("Crows-an-Carn", by the way, was also a name given to a small iron mine, officially South Mount, close to the road a little further west.) The quarry was linked to the Treamble branch by its own tramway, which was carried over the stream, supported by the two brick walls which still stand beside it. The main access to Treamble Mine at one time was a road or track which crossed the stream at about the same point.

❺ **At the T-junction turn left. Go over the bridge, through the gate, across the farmyard of Stampas Farm, and bear right. Go through the open gateway on the right (following the yellow arrow) on to a path between hedges, and turn right again at the waymark post.** This is another attractive path, but often extremely muddy on both sides of the stream, although there are a few helpful - if uneven and insecure - stepping-stones. A set of water-powered Cornish stamps once worked here - hence the name of the farm you have just passed. Mr Glanville believes that the tin ore for stamping came from a mine called Wheal Thomas, a few hundred yards to the east at Hendra farm, and also probably from Mount and Rejerrah mines. No written records of Wheal Thomas seem to have survived, but it is said to have produced a little lead as well as tin, and to have ceased operations before 1830. **After the stone footbridge you will pass Primrose Cottage,** and the drive leading up from there was indeed a mass of primroses in March. **Cross two cattle-grids.**

Immediately after the first one, look down on the left to see Rosewater fishing lake, which was excavated in about 1989. Until about a century ago, Stampas corn mill stood down there, and its millpool occupied part of what is now the lake. **At the T-junction turn right, then left, through a gate, before the farm buildings at Hendravossan.** This is an interesting name, because the last part derives from the Cornish *fosyn* meaning "dykes" in the sense of walls, thus suggesting that some kind of ancient fortification or boundary wall once stood on or near its land. See also the note on Gear Sands. **The farm track curves to the right before reaching the road via a gate.**

❻ **Turn right, and when you reach the coast road go straight across: there is a public footpath sign. Take the most definite path, which cuts its way among gorse bushes and heads across Gear Sands (*) towards the sea - not left, towards Perran Sands Holiday Village and Perranporth. The white-painted stones are very helpful on this part of the walk, where there are so few distinctive features by which to give directions. Where they divide into two lines, follow the ones bearing right, which will eventually bring you to an ancient Cornish cross.** Close to this was the site of the original Perranzabuloe parish church. A short way north-east of the cross is the openwork pit or quarry which is the most obvious relic of Halwyn iron mine. The small manor of Halwyn appears in the Domesday Book as "Elhil". The name Halwyn, common in Cornwall, normally means "white hall", but Henderson suggested a different interpretation, as mentioned in the note on Ellenglaze. Mr Roger Glanville tells me he has noticed traces of buildings and boundary hedges near the pit; whether these relate to the ancient manor, or the mine, or neither, I do not know.

GEAR SANDS

The sands take their name, I presume, from Gear Farm, a short way to the east, and the name of the farm derives from the Cornish word "ker", a round. Gear Farm is very close to Hendravossan, so both names may refer to the same ancient fortification. St Piran's Round lies only a short way south, and could be the one both farm names allude to, but Mr Roger Glanville believes there were three such structures in close proximity. St Piran's Round is included in Walk 3 and as a short diversion in Walk 6.

❼ **Now head left, towards the tall cross in the distance.** (This is made of concrete, and was erected in 1969 to help people searching for St Piran's Oratory (*). The story of its manufacture and how the 40-ton object was moved into position by means of a tank-retrieving vehicle is told by Bill Trembath.) **Still follow the white stones, crossing a stream in a deep hollow**: the one small stepping-stone was needed in January, but I suspect the stream may dry up in some summers. **After this the stones led through quite a deep pond** - also a temporary phenomenon, I suspect, although this little reservoir of fresh water probably explains the choice of site for the Oratory. **Even in winter it was easy enough to get around the pool, on the right side, and to reach the steep little path with wooden step-boards** which runs up the side of the artificial sandhill beneath which the Oratory nestles, supposedly safe now from the elements and the vandals. **Now take the wide path heading towards the sea, steering just left of the signs warning you to keep out of the Penhale military area.**

ST PIRAN'S ORATORY, CROSS AND CHURCH

This seems to be what happened here, so far as can be deduced from the surviving evidence:

In the late 6th century Celtic "missionaries" from Ireland, among whom was a man who has come to be known as St Piran (usually said as "Pirran", though the local pronunciation, "Pyran", seems closer to the early spelling, "Pieran"), established a monastic settlement called Lanpiran or Lamberran near a spring on this site, probably including a small "oratory" or chapel, a school, a refectory, cells for the abbot and monks and a cemetery. All the buildings are likely to have been of wattle and daub or timber. A tall granite cross (8ft 10in high) was erected at the eastern boundary. We know this was in place by 960, apparently a little further inland than it is now. (See page 50 for more about the cross.) By that time the original oratory had been replaced by a simple stone building 29ft long and 16ft 6in wide (25ft by 12ft, according to some sources, perhaps referring to internal measurements). During the following centuries periodic flooding tended to damage the oratory, and the shifting sands always threatened to engulf it, so it seems that by about 1100 another oratory was built on higher ground near the cross, and in about 1150 the decision was taken to build a new, larger church (usually referred to now as the Norman church) on the same site. The old oratory was apparently abandoned, but never truly the "Lost Church" it has been nicknamed: the shifting sands would bury it, then reveal it again. Lanpiran or "St Piran in the Sands" (=Perranzabuloe) became an important shrine, visited by many pilgrims. The "holy relics" on show included a casket that supposedly held St Piran's head. By the 18th century even the Norman church was under threat from the sands (partly, it is said, because tinners had been allowed to divert the stream which till then had helped keep the sand back), and in 1804 work was begun on building yet another church, this time well away from the dunes at Lambourne (see Walk 4). The Norman church was finally abandoned the following year. Much of the 12th-century building was used in constructing the new one. At this time the ancient oratory was visible, but before long it seems to have been buried again. Archaeological digs took place in 1835 and 1843. A headless skeleton, one of three reportedly found under the altar in 1835, was that of an unusually tall man;

tradition had it that St Piran was very tall, so the obvious conclusion was drawn - but few if any modern scholars would confidently support it. Early this century there was further excavation, and in 1910 an ugly concrete-block shelter was built around the oratory, though still allowing access for visitors and occasional services.

Damage from flooding and vandalism still occurred, and in 1980 it was decided that the only practicable way to ensure its survival was to cover it with the sands once more. The site of the Norman church was excavated in 1917-9, when the chancel walls were found to be almost complete; but that, too, is safely tucked away under the dunes now.

"Beneath this stone is buried the Oratory...."

The story is told in more detail by Bill Trembath and especially by E.W.F. Tomlin.

❽ Before long you will reach the beach below, and even if the tide is high you should be able to turn right on that. Soon you will see a large red notice beneath the low cliffs, a warning from the Cornwall County Council about the rigours of the walk ahead, but please don't let it put you off! On the other hand, it must be stressed again that the path around the cliff-edge ahead could be dangerous in rough weather, and those who suffer from vertigo might be well advised to avoid it even in calm conditions.

At the bottom of the cliffs can be found the mouth of the adit that drained a small mine called Wheal Mary, whose buildings once stood among the dunes north-west of the Oratory. Dines (1953) called this "an old tin and copper mine", but Hamilton Jenkin, ten years later, referred to five shafts that developed two lead lodes.

There is a big variety of attractive pebbles and stones on the beach, but the further you go the more common become the rough-shaped fragments which look like bits of rusty iron - and in this case, appearances do not deceive. Just where the high cliffs start, at the end of the beach, you should be able to make out a reddish-brown streak in the rock, immediately

below the point where there has been quarrying on the top of the cliff. Walk up to the foot of the cliff here to see the impressive caverns and shafts created by miners working this outcrop of the Great Perran Iron Lode (*). The mine here was called Gravel Hill. This is a place of special interest to geologists: when my wife and I were last there, a group of them were busy searching for traces of a rare, bright-green crystalline iron compound. (Bill Trembath mentions "rare phosphates of iron called ferro-strunzite, beraunite, and eleonirite.")

THE GREAT PERRAN IRON LODE

"The Vein has been worked formerly, and is vastly large," wrote John Woodward in about 1720. It runs inland to the south-east for at least three miles and was worked by several mines, including Gravel Hill, Halwyn, Mount (whose small stack is a prominent landmark on the inland part of this walk), Treamble and Duchy Peru (south of Rejerrah). "During the 1860s," writes Hamilton Jenkin, "the ore was drawn up the cliff from the seaward workings of Gravel Hill by a 11½ in. 'puffer' engine, whence it was carted a distance of three miles to a newly constructed quay on the Gannel for shipment." The engine house and separate stack were still substantially intact in 1937, as shown by a photograph in H.G.Ordish's first volume (page 52). J.H.Collins describes the iron ore as "low-grade", and none of these mines, except perhaps Duchy Peru, was ever a great financial success, despite the fact that a good deal of zinc was recovered along with the haematite. The Cornwall Minerals Railway brought a line to Treamble during the 1870s, but in the event the traffic in iron ore proved a disappointment. Some open-cast iron mining was still being done at Treamble in the 1930s, and it was operated by the British Iron and Steel Corporation during the Second World War.

❾ Go up the very steep path just to the right of the iron lode. When the mine was working a small steam engine at the cliff-edge hauled the ore up a skip-road or tramway which occupied approximately the course of this path. **Follow the acorn signs past a concrete-capped shaft and the open-cast workings of Gravel Hill mine.** As you head towards Ligger Point there is a superb view of the huge beach and past the pair of islets known as the Bawden Rocks, Cow and Calf or the Man and his Man ("man" probably deriving from the Cornish word, "maen", a stone or rock) to the cliffs as far west as Pendeen Watch (near Cape Cornwall) in very clear conditions. Soon you will see several capped, fenced-off mineshafts, relics of the Penhale Mine (*).

THE PENHALE MINE AND WHEAL GOLDEN

Four lead lodes which are also rich in silver have been found in the area round these headlands. Some copper and iron are also present. The workings go back in time well beyond existing records; by the early 19th century, three mines were operating: Penhale, at Ligger Point, Wheal Golden or Golding at Penhale Point, and East Wheal Golden, further inland. Surveys done in about 1850 revealed, writes Hamilton Jenkin, "upwards of 3,000 fathoms of drives and stopes, and 13 old men's shafts." As with so many other Cornish mines, these were shut down and re-opened according to the fluctuations of metal prices; for example, they closed in the mid-1820s; Penhale re-opened in 1830 but gave poor results; and in 1848 all three mines were amalgamated as Wheal Golden Consols. The deepest shaft at Penhale Point began yielding copiously, and rather than transport all the ore to the Gannel and Padstow, as before, the company bought a small ship and built a landing-bay on the cliff slope on the Holywell Beach side of the headland, remains of which can still be seen. The whim engine was adapted for use in raising coal up the cliff face. During the winter of 1851-2, the sea broke into the Penhale Mine's workings, and the cost of repairing the breach used up all the mine's profits. In 1867, Penhale was started up again as Penhale and Lomax, and much building was done on the Ligger headland, including that of the count-house which still remains. By 1870, the workings had reached a depth of about 800 feet and there was a workforce of 200. When the army took over the area as Penhale Camp during the Second World War, the Penhale and Wheal Golden engine houses still dominated their headlands, but the military authorities, in Hamilton Jenkin's phrase, "wantonly demolished" them. This followed an air-raid on Penhale Camp in 1940; it was held that the old buildings were too convenient a landmark for enemy bombers. The Wheal Golden building had been particularly prominent and distinctive, and Ordish's 1934 photograph of it (page 55 in his 1967 book) shows how similar it was to the Wheal Ellen engine house in the Porthtowan valley (Walk 8). Ordish refers to its "greenish-black clay-slate, with its bright red-brick castellated stack".

The house on the ridge above - seen more clearly after you have rounded Ligger Point - was once the mine's count house. H. G. Ordish's first book includes four fine 1930s photos of Penhale Mine. **The coastal footpath, marked by a series of posts, keeps near the cliff-edge and goes round Ligger Point**, after which you have your first view of the sheer cliffs around Hoblyn's Cove, which somehow for me are made the more forbidding by the signs of all the work done on, in and under them by miners and others over the centuries. One of the great arches cut in the rock certainly looks man-made, with its unusually square top. There is an old shaft at the point where the wooden fencing on the edge of Penhale military camp begins, and later several more, two of which are right by the cliff edge.

Penhale Mine, Ligger Point, at a time when the pumping engine had been removed but the whim engine was still in place. The pumping-engine house was built for an 80-inch engine, but a 66-inch from Violet Seton Mine, Camborne, was installed. Since the "woodwork of the house" went with it, the window-frames were slightly too small for the openings in the masonry, so brick infill was used around the frames, giving the house a unique appearance.

Imagine being a miner who perhaps walked here each morning from Holywell or even from Rose -as many did - often in a howling gale, climbed down near-vertical ladders to a depth which by 1870 had reached nearly 800 feet, worked in cramped, damp and probably hot conditions for eight hours, and at last struggled up again "to grass".... Roger Glanville informs me in a letter, "Phil Penna of Hendravossan (who became President of the United Mine Workers of America) and Josiah Osborne from Rose (who became Captain of the Horn Silver Mine in Frisco, Utah) both record in their memoirs that at the age of 10 (in the late 1860s) they worked in Wheal Mary and Penhale, and went up and down these ladders attached to their fathers with a length of rope tied round their waists. They even describe the sound of the sea crashing on the shore above them."

Keep following the white posts. As you approach the first of the large fenced circles surrounding "non-ionising radiation" masts at the Royal Navy Wireless Station, look back at the sinister black cliff-face to see a couple of pieces of timber which perhaps once supported a platform and staircase leading down to the shaft entrance a few feet below; or was there formerly a horsewhim on the flattish area near the cliff edge? The view inland includes Cubert church spire, the windmills at Carland Cross, and further left the china-clay "mountains" near St Austell.

The path continues round Penhale Point, the area mined by Wheal Golden; there is also evidence of a prehistoric settlement here. The view along the coast that has revealed itself now stretches to the lighthouse at Trevose Head near Padstow. The remains can still be discerned of a landing-bay constructed by the mines on the east side of Penhale Point so that ships could deliver coal for the engines.

Now you turn inland, towards Holywell; the path follows, at least in part, the course of a mine tramway. What looks like a concrete shaft-cap with iron hoops at the cliff edge is in fact used by the Army for rock-climbing and abseiling exercises.

As you reach Holywell, the St Piran's Inn, as previously mentioned, is just by the path, and a little way up the road is the Treguth Inn, which occupies an old farmhouse, claimed to date from the 13th century. (John N. Rosewarne's selection of old photographs, *Bygone Cornwall*, published by D. Bradford Barton in 1970, includes one of Treguth Farm in the days before the motor-car invaded Cornwall, when the farmer's cows "were able to seek shade and coolness on the beach." Even at that time, though, "real Cornish teas" were served at the farmhouse. Its name probably means "farm of the hollow or enclosure".) There are also shops and cafés.

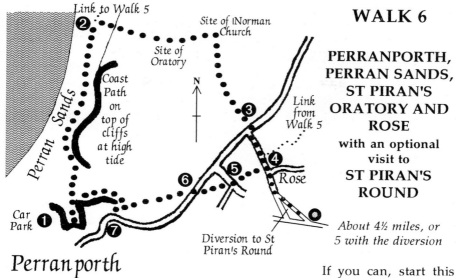

WALK 6

PERRANPORTH, PERRAN SANDS, ST PIRAN'S ORATORY AND ROSE

with an optional visit to

ST PIRAN'S ROUND

About 4½ miles, or 5 with the diversion

Perran porth

If you can, start this walk when the tide is fairly low and still on the way out; otherwise you will be unable to inspect some interesting caves, many of which bear evidence of mining activity. It would be helpful to bring a torch if you want to look for that. At high tide you will have to start the walk on the cliffs rather than the beach. The suggested route repeats, in the opposite direction, the path across Gear Sands, visiting the site of St Piran's Oratory, which is included in Walk 5. This is quite an easy walk, except that Perran Sands can be a little too soft for comfortable walking, and there is a fairly steep climb up the sandhills when you turn inland, if you have come along the beach. Perranporth has toilets, shops and pubs.

NOTE: Directions are given at the end for combining Walks 5 and 6 into one route of just over ten miles, omitting Gear Sands and the Oratory.

Directions for driving to Perranporth (*) are given for Walk 7. This walk, too, starts at the main car park.

PERRANPORTH
When locals say the name they put the stress on the last syllable. Perranporth and the parish of Perranzabuloe (Latin, "in sabulo": in the sand) take their name from the 6th-century saint Piran, who arrived in this part of Cornwall from Ireland rather unconventionally, floating on a millstone to which he had been tied by heathens before being thrown over a cliff into a stormy sea. (Those of a down-to-earth disposition may prefer the theory that the "millstone" was actually a small

altar of the sort that many such early saints are said to have taken around with them.) Several places in the county are dedicated to him, notably a chapel at Tintagel in the east, the church at Perranuthnoe in the west, and the inland parish of Perranarworthal south-west of Truro. He is the patron saint of the tinners, having been credited with the discovery of tin, or with teaching the miners the art of smelting. The Cornish flag or banner, St Piran's Cross, is said to represent "the light of the gospel shining in a world of sin" and to depict the cross he made from molten white tin. Since for centuries it was mining alone - apart from pilchard seining - that supported the population of Perranporth, its patron saint is a fitting one. Tin was produced, but also lead, silver, zinc and especially copper. "Miles of galleries lie beneath the village," writes Bill Trembath, who gives a vivid account of what the place must have looked, sounded and smelt like when the two principal mines - Great Wheal Leisure in the centre and to the east, Perran Great St George to the west - were active. The drawing, based on one of the earliest Cornish photographs (probably about 1850), shows (to the left and in the foreground) the two engine houses of Wheal Leisure, already ruined by about 1850. They originally contained pumping engines with 70- and 66-inch cylinders. Between 1827 and 1840, this mine sold nearly 52,000 tons of copper ore. Both mines closed early in the 1870s, after years of bitter territorial disputes, but there is valuable metal still to be had in these rocks. Not long after that, the great shoals of pilchards suddenly deserted the Cornish coasts. Although the holiday trade as we understand it began in earnest here only after the arrival of the railway in 1903, Perranporth had been a favourite day-trip destination for Truronians as much as a century earlier. By the latter part of the 19th century sea-bathing at Perranporth was sufficiently popular for segregation of the sexes to be deemed necessary on the western beach: gentlemen bathers only till 9 am, ladies only from 9 till midday!

Perranporth has a folk museum and an information centre, both well worth visiting; for information about them, see the end of the directions for Walk 7.

❶ Go over the bridge on the right (as you look out to sea) side of the car park. Notice the "caves" - one of which is bricked up - in the low cliff on the right. Like so many of the holes in the cliffs around Perranporth, it is hard to tell which are natural and which man-made, but the whole area around and under the village is riddled with mine workings.

Cross the second bridge and head north towards the distant headland, Ligger Point, which marks the end of the two-mile stretch of Perran Sands. On your right you will see how the sand-dunes are being planted with marram grass to stabilise them; without that they are nearly as mobile as the sea, and much evidence of the miners' activities in these parts is now buried under the sand.

Soon you will reach an outcrop of cliffs, and if the tide is against you you will have to climb the path to the top of these, following the acorn signs; even so, you may be able to look into one or two of the caves first, and work out which if any of these holes are mine adits.

A typical cave near Perranporth

The little one on the right of the steps is certainly man-made, for example, and the first sizeable cave to the left contains the mouths of two adits, one of which is on the right soon after you enter. The small cave after that seems to have a narrow drainage shaft in the roof .... and so on: if you have the time to explore them all, and especially if you brought a torch, there are plenty of opportunities for detective work - and even those not yet bitten by the bug will have to agree that many of the larger caves are impressive enough to be worth a look. Some display beautiful, glistening rock-strata and amazingly vivid stains caused by the minerals in the dripping water, and the force of the tide is shown not only by the stacks of driftwood at the far ends of deep caves, but also by the bits of debris lodged high up in side-clefts. The holes, usually square-sided, a few feet up the cliff-face are almost certainly adits, set above high-tide mark. Near the end of the stretch of high cliffs is an adit mouth (Wheal Byan Adit) at beach level with a steady flow of water issuing from it. These workings were parts of several small mines; the closest to Perranporth were Wheal Ramoth (pronounced "Raymoth") and North Leisure, and most of the others at two periods were grouped under the name of Perran Consols (*). The lower cliffs that follow show much less, if any, evidence of mining; then follows a large area of dunes. The pebbles on the beach are exceptionally attractive, and their very varied colouring hints at the complexity of the rock formations nearby.

(By the way, I recommend Bill Trembath's account of the walk along Perran Sands [pages 87-9]: the details he provides about the locality and its wildlife would, I think, add greatly to your enjoyment of this section.)

PERRAN CONSOLS

There were at least six ancient mines here: Wheal Creeg, Wheal Vlow (pronounced to rhyme with "how"), Wheal Widden, Wheal Mary, Wheal Hope, Rose Mine and Budnick; Vlow was "worked for tin before 1750" according to J.H.Collins, and records of Creeg go back to 1774. Their main shafts and buildings were about half a mile inland. From 1835 to 1840 they were amalgamated as Perran Consolidated and employed a hundred people. The title was revived in the 1870s, when Wheal Vlow's shafts were taken down to 240 feet below the level of the adit, and this mine was prospected again in 1927, but without success. Wheal Mary lay a little further north than the route of this walk; some details about that are given in Walk 5. (In Winston Graham's "Poldark" novels, the mine Ross owned at the end of the 18th century could well have been based on one of this group. Bill Trembath says Wheal Vlow was his model, but that he confused matters by naming the fictional mine after another one nearby, Wheal Leisure. Incidentally, the name "Nampara", also made famous by "Poldark", is that of a group of cottages near St Michael's Church in Perranporth; locals pronounce it "Namperra".)

❷ **For the longer route, including Holywell, stay on the beach** and refer to the instructions at the end of the directions for this walk. **To find St Piran's Oratory, you need to climb the sandy slope near the far end of the area of dunes just mentioned - that is, just before a few more rocky outcrops show through, and keeping to the right of the signs warning you to stay clear of the military area. Continue ahead along the obvious path, always keeping the warning signs close on your left.** Soon you will see the tall concrete cross intended to guide people to the Oratory. The sandy hillock under which the latter is buried is fairly near the cross, but further left and at a lower level; a granite slab marks the spot. **From there, a line of white-painted stones marks the way to the old cross near the site of the medieval Church of St Piran, and continues south across Gear Sands to meet the coast road.** All this part of the route is described in reverse direction in Walk 5, which has notes on the Oratory, the Church and Gear Sands.

❸ (If you want to get back to Perranporth by the most direct route, you could turn right and follow the coast road till you reach the path on the right at point 6. Even out of season, however, this road can be quite busy, so I would recommend the following route, keeping to minor roads and paths.) **Cross the coast road and continue almost straight ahead along the minor road into Rose village.** (There is a note about Rose in Walk 3.)

❹ **Just past the telephone kiosk take the public footpath on the right.**
(But if you would like to include a visit to St Piran's Round, a short diversion at this point - about a quarter of a mile each way - will bring you to it. For that, continue ahead, past the chapel. The original chapel was in fact the building on the right, now converted into a private house, and the present chapel started life as the Sunday School, at a time when there were 120 pupils! This gives some measure of the extent to which the village population has declined since the heyday of mining in this locality. Go on past the left turning to Lower Rose, and just before you reach the tiny post office fork left on to a byway that leads straight to the Round. See Walk 3 for information about it. Return the same way, taking the footpath on the left just before the phone box.)
After the gate, go straight across the field, then through the kissing-gate and up a few steps at the field corner. Near the end of the field, there are shafts in the gorse-patch on the left. These are Bice's Shafts, part of Budnick Mine (see Walk 3, section 9). On the right of the path at the top of the steps is the former site of the mine's dressing floors (now overgrown).

❺ **At the road, turn right, ignore the left turning and cross the stile with a metal bar over it at the corner.** The ruins of Bice's engine house can be seen on the left as you cross this stile, about 100 yards away. **Now the**

path runs diagonally across the field and heads straight for the centre of Perranporth. Soon it brings you back to the coast road.

❻ Cross that and continue in exactly the same line, heading for Perranporth across the golf course, following the line of posts. Eventually the path joins a little tarmacked road; some steps down to the left and a sandy path bring you to the main road.

❼ Turn right and immediately right again, over a stile next to a green gate, and follow the river round to the two bridges and the car park.

TO COMBINE PARTS OF WALKS 5 & 6

A fine all-day ramble with refreshments conveniently available at the start/end and half-way points can easily be created from these two routes by omitting the section common to both, across Gear Sands. If you start the walk at Perranporth, continue along Perran Sands at point 2 in Walk 6 and pick up the directions at point 7 in Walk 5. Carry on with Walk 5, covering points 7, 8, 1, 2, 3 and 4. At point 5 turn left instead of right, and complete the walk from Rose village, reading from point 4 in Walk 6. You could, of course, equally well make Holywell your start/end point.

The old cross in the dunes, now a useful guide to the site of the Norman church of Perranzabuloe. Only one other Cornish cross - at Egloshayle, Wadebridge - has three holes right through the head. Arthur Langdon in *Old Cornish Crosses* (1896) noted even a century ago that little decorative carving remained on it; he thought that "the action of sand driven by the wind" was a likely explanation.

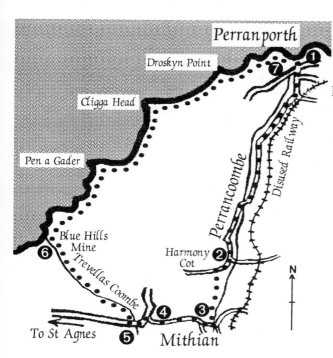

WALK 7

PERRANPORTH, PERRANCOOMBE, MITHIAN, TREVELLAS COOMBE AND THE COAST

About 7½ miles

Another very fine walk, beginning this time inland, mostly by valley streams. The coastal section starts with an extremely steep climb and continues quite strenuous, so allow extra time. Plan the walk, if possible, so that the tide is low when you get back to Perranporth; you can then explore the area of ancient mining in the cliffs at the west end of the beach. No-one staying in this area should miss "Jericho Valley". Most of the inland walking is on roads, but these are usually quiet apart from one short stretch. The path following point 2 on the map is often muddy. A pleasant pub, the Miners Arms, is very conveniently placed at Mithian.

The walk begins from the main car park in Perranporth, overlooking the beach. To drive there from St Agnes, take the B3285 eastwards; from Truro, take the A390 westwards to Chiverton Cross roundabout, turn right on to the A3075 (Newquay) road, turning left for Perranporth where signposted.
See Walk 6 for a note about Perranporth.

❶ **We start with the inland section of the route, so walk back past the Tywarnhayle (called "The Village Pub"), cross the bridge and go past Lloyds Bank and Boscawen Park** (given by Lord Falmouth, whose family name is Boscawen), **following the signs to Perrancoombe.** Notice the remains of the railway bridge at the corner, part of the Chacewater to Newquay loop line, described in notes on other walks. **A pleasant short** path has been created along the top of the embankment, so I suggest you go up the steps and continue as far as possible, then return to the valley road and turn left.

Immediately after passing a large pine tree on the right, look down close to the road on that side and you will see a buddle, a circular pit, probably nearly full of water, with a raised central part. This is of 20th century origin, probably the relic of a streamwork or a small enterprise recovering ore from old mine burrows. A small mine called Wheal Friendship or Wheal Blandford, which was working in the 1830s, was on the steep slope on the opposite side of the stream.

Where the main road curves left, keep straight on, signed to Leycroft. After the bridge over the stream and the nearby pump, which looks very well cared for, the valley becomes more rural and much more attractive. This is Carnbargus (which seems to mean "the rock-pile of the kite"). A little further on, the disturbed ground on the gorse-covered slopes to the right suggests another old mine, and indeed this is the site of Prince Royal (*).

PRINCE ROYAL MINE

"Never much of a mine, although it appears to have possibilities," wrote J.H.Collins in 1912. It sold 206 tons of copper ore in 1825-6, a little tin in 1887, and seemed to have some promising lead deposits. The mine was also, at various times, called Princess Royal and Prince Albert Consols; unfortunately, these expressions of loyalty to the monarchy don't seem to have been rewarded by much commercial success.

❷ Where you join another road, near a ford, keep straight on, signposted to St Agnes. To continue the walk, turn left a few yards later on a path signposted to Mithian; but first it's worth walking about a hundred yards further along the road to see the attractive thatched cottage called Harmony Cot, birthplace of John Opie (*). (This district is still called "Blowinghouse" - the term in Cornwall for the early type of tin-smelting works which employed a bellows, usually powered by a waterwheel, to raise the furnace temperature - and the Opies' cottage was called "The Blowing House" until John's first wife, Mary, made him change it. A stream which could have been harnessed for the waterwheel runs close to the cottage. Prettier the new name may have been, but it must have developed ironic overtones in the following years, during which he neglected her until finally she ran off with a Major. By 1874 the name had been changed again, to "Woodcocks"; when it reverted to "Harmony Cot" I don't know.)

WALK 7

JOHN OPIE

Born in 1761, the son of a mine carpenter-cum-builder, John or "Jan" Opie was a multi-talented man, a mathematician and philosopher who earned the nickname "little Sir Isaac", but it was as a portrait painter that he achieved fame and a second nickname, "The Cornish Wonder". John Wolcot, a Truro doctor and satirical writer better known by his pseudonym "Peter Pindar", "discovered" Opie, gave help and encouragement, and in 1781 took him to London, introducing him to the people who mattered in the art world. He exhibited 143 pictures at the Royal Academy in London, and produced in all about 750 paintings as well as many illustrations, especially of Shakespeare. He died aged only 45, poisoned, some said, by the lead in his paints. Following a lavish funeral, in which his hearse, drawn by six black horses, was followed by 59 other coaches of mourners, he was buried in the crypt of St Paul's Cathedral. The St Agnes Museum has a John Opie display, which includes one of his paintboxes, and the acquisition of an Opie self-portrait by the Museum Trust was announced in February 1994. In the Royal Cornwall Museum at Truro is a particularly interesting example of his work, entitled "Gentleman and a Miner". Painted in 1786, it is essentially a portrait of Thomas Daniell, the father of "Guinea-a-Minute Daniell": see the notes on Wheal Towan in the next walk and on the Mansion House (Truro) in Walk 12 of "A Second View from Carn Marth".

From Harmony Cot return to the Mithian footpath, crossing the twin stiles and passing just to the left of an old barn. On the opposite side of the valley is the site of one of several mines in Cornwall called Wheal Prosper, worked in a small way in the 1820s. In 1852 it was restarted under the name Perran Wheal Alfred with a 30-inch pumping engine, but this working was short lived.

After a gate the path continues close to the stream, and you are likely to encounter plenty of sticky mud, but this is a delightful spot where sheep graze on steeply-sloping pasture above. Steps take you into a wooded stretch, and soon you will reach a small group of ruined buildings, the remains of a cottage and the site of an old grist mill. A photograph in Clive Benney's earlier volume shows Mithian Old Mill as it was in about 1906. Among the trees on the far side of the valley, as you approach the road, is the imposing Georgian manor house called Rose-in-Vale, now a hotel and restaurant but formerly the home of John Oates, owner of Wheal Leisure, the mine on the east side of Perranporth.

❸ At the road, notice the former mill opposite, where despite renovation it still seems possible to trace the outline of the waterwheel on the facing wall. **Here turn right into Mithian (*). At the Miners Arms, turn right and continue up the road, heading towards St Agnes Beacon.**

WALK 7

MITHIAN

A settlement called "Mithien" appears in a document dated 1201. The name, as Padel says, looks Cornish, but its origin and meaning are unknown. One of the plaster ceilings in the Miners Arms bears the date 1577; the pub also has its "secret passage", linking it to the manor house opposite (now converted into five small dwellings) - or rather it used to have, since much of the tunnel has now collapsed. Mithian Church was built in the middle of the 19th century; the original spire was destroyed by lightning in 1898 and eventually replaced by a tower built of stone taken from an old engine house. Please don't waste your time searching Mithian for the church: it's three miles away, near the Chiverton Cross roundabout. (It might, however, be worth looking for the remains of the old church, which according to John King "stood at the head of the village". He says that small louvre windows and an arched doorway from it are "now incorporated in farm buildings.") Mithian's tiny post office is also quite a way from the village centre (at or near Barkla Shop); when I originally researched this book there was also a general store near the pub, but that has gone now. "Mithian," says the WI's Cornwall Village Book, "once boasted a bakery, a tailor, a shoemaker, three shops .... (and) .... a Methodist chapel"; now they exist only in the memory, like the mines which provided employment, and Mithian Halt, on the railway line that closed in 1963. Wheal Prosper to the north and Wheals Mithian, Liberty, Valley and Frederick to the south were the closest mines, but they had finished by the middle of the 19th century.

❹ **Turn left at the T-junction. Please take care on this busy road. Ignore the left turning where the main road bends right; continue down to Barkla Shop,** the small group of houses where the stream flowing down Trevellas Coombe crosses the road. "Shop" refers to a smithy, named after the blacksmith: "Barkla" was once a common surname hereabouts.

❺ **Turn right on to the path just past the bridge - a pretty, wooded walk by the stream. When you come to a wider track, bear right.** In the area just behind you at this point - that is, in the triangle formed by the road, the path you came on and the wider track - was Jericho Stamps (*).

JERICHO STAMPS

West Kitty mined the tin beneath St Agnes village and could not set up dressing floors there, so all the ore had to be transported by horse-and-cart to Trevellas Coombe. The cost of the two-mile haul eventually contributed to the mine's downfall. In this quiet spot now it is hard to imagine the activity, grime and racket which must have surrounded the quite large industrial complex shown in my drawing, which is based on an undated postcard. If you want to try to relate the scene in the picture to what's there now, go a little way up the slope on the left as you approach the gateway to Jericho Cottage and look back up the valley. Half-

hidden among the trees and undergrowth are the remains of many buildings, some of them quite substantial; now that nature has taken over again so completely, it seems amazing that Jericho Stamps was still a going concern well into the 20th century. J.A.Buckley's "Cornish Mining - at Surface" has an amazing photograph of it, dating from around 1900. The still substantial ruins on the site in 1925 are shown in a photograph in Clive Benney's later volume. ("One cylinder bolt of the stamps engine is still visible!" Kenneth Brown tells me.) I have not come across an explanation of "Jericho"(sometimes spelt "Jerico"), but many Cornish places were given Biblical names in the time of men like Billy Bray, the miner-evangelist from Twelveheads, near Bissoe: Bethel and Salem are two other examples, and "Promised Land" is about a mile from here. Trevellas Coombe is commonly known as Jericho Valley.

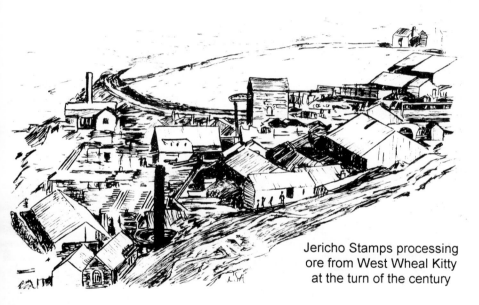

Jericho Stamps processing
ore from West Wheal Kitty
at the turn of the century

As indicated by the footpath sign, cross the footbridge, then keep left near the stream, passing beside Jericho Cottage, which was built on or close to the site of a burning house. Soon after this you will see a small heap of mine waste on the other bank of the stream, and if you look to your right at the same point you will find the portal of an adit, now bricked up. As the valley opens out towards the sea, evidence of tin streaming, as well as lode mining, grows more and more obvious. On the left just before you reach the fishponds are the remains of a twelve-headed stamps machine, once driven by a waterwheel: the leat is still there. Six of the stamps' "lifters" remain, and on the big axle can be seen the cams which raised them and let them drop on the ore. Also visible are the ratchet teeth to stop them running backwards and being damaged. A few yards further on, a dismantled waterwheel was, when I was last there, propped against the wall beneath the track. This was bought from Penzance about 1984 or 1985 and there are hopes that it will eventually be rebuilt and work elsewhere in St Agnes parish. Tin streaming and smelting are still carried out by members of the Wills family in this part of Trevellas Coombe, although while tin prices remain low the family also need other occupations such as fish farming. Lower down the valley, you will see the entrance of a level shaft beside the engine house; it has been blocked off after about 30 feet. The ruined mine buildings (several of which have recently been repointed by Carrick District Council), the burrows and the shafts are relics of Blue Hills Mine. This tin mine was active, although not working continuously, between 1813 and 1898, but there were many smaller workings here at least as far back as the 18th century, and there are records of stamping mills in the valley in 1693. The lodes being worked were mined by Goonlaze and Penhalls Mines and Wheal Kitty a little further west, and they are all linked underground. The engine house was built for a 70-inch pumping engine; the shaft beside its bob wall has been filled in, but the balance-bob pit is still visible.

A view up Trevellas Coombe, about 1890. The stack and pumping-engine house of Blue Hills Mine are still there. To the left of the flywheel are the stamps, driven by a horizontal engine which could also hoist from several shafts.

When you reach the road, bear right; the lower track gives you the better view of the stack and the pit near it. The pit was constructed for the flywheel of a whim and stamps engine. Near the edge of the low cliff are yet more mine buildings. (For fuller details of the mining remains at the seaward end of this valley, see the Cornwall Archaeological Unit's study, mentioned in the Further Reading list, and the forthcoming Landfall book, "Exploring Cornwall's Mines".) If you care to scramble down to the beach you will be able to look more closely at the mouth of an adit, where water is flowing out quite near the notice warning of dangerous currents.

❻ Now you have a stiff climb up the hillside on the right, following the coastal footpath back to Perranporth. Take the middle one of the three footpaths (though Roger Radcliffe tells me that Cornwall County Council has worked on these paths, "and a single route is now advocated"). Waymark posts are placed near the top. There is a capped shaft high up on the right. **Keep to the main path, which soon heads a little inland - although you could walk round the headland if you wish.** Now you are faced by spectacular red cliffs, whose contorted strata give some idea of the mineral richness of the land hereabouts. The green stains, very bright on some of the cliffs between here and Perranporth, are evidence of copper. A tiny waterfall issues from the cliff-face, and when my wife and I were last there a gale blew all the water inland, providing a shower-bath as we walked by the cliff-edge above it. Next the path runs through part of a World War II airfield, created in 1940; the odd-looking bunkers were built in order to provide shelter from the winds for the rather flimsy aircraft, according to Bill Trembath; I have also been told that they were gun emplacements. (The Trevellas airfield has been used since the late '50s mainly by a gliding club. It has been the focus of much controversy in the period between the first and second editions of this book because of plans by its owners to increase greatly the number of aircraft using it.) Soon after this, just past Pen a Gader ("headland of the chair or seat"; "Grader" on some O.S. maps is a misprint), there are shafts near the cliff-edge, and a hole near the foot of the cliff looks like an adit; these are probably workings of Wheal Prudence (*).

WHEAL PRUDENCE
"A very ancient mine," says Collins. Recorded sales of copper go back to 1812, but some of the adits whose mouths are scattered everywhere on the hillsides and cliff-faces on this stretch of coast are much older than that, and Prudence was really a group of older mines with such names as Hanover Cove, Wheal Jacka, Wheal Cock and Wheal Meadow. About 1826, Prudence was bought by a London company and amalgamated with Cligga and Great St George mines; this enterprise closed in 1839, but in 1862 a house for a 70-inch pumping engine was erected and

a new shaft sunk, about 100 yards inland, to a depth of about 700 feet. (To help you imagine that: the mine's adit, issuing at the bottom of the cliff, was 300 feet "below grass".) " 'The failure of the last working,' explained the Mining Journal 15th November 1862, 'was due to the unjudicious attempt to work the sea-ward lodes by direct workings from a detached and storm-beaten island rock instead of by a cross-cut.' On this prominence was sunk the Island Shaft which can only be approached today by a crumbling knife-edged path, bordered on one side by the awe-inspiring chasm of the 'Old Prison' and on the other by the scarcely less sheer cliffs of Cocking's Cove." (A.K.H.Jenkin: "Mines and Miners of Cornwall") The miners reached the island by means of a wooden bridge, the site of which can still be seen. In February 1863 the Mining Journal reported that "the resident agent....and the engineers....have displayed much energy in getting such an amount of work done in the winter months in such a situation....exposed to the full sweep of the Atlantic so that during the north-westerly gales spray from the waves frequently flew over the engine-house, driving the workmen from their posts." In the following years, however, the costs involved in undersea mining proved a problem, and the mine closed in 1868. Collins mentions "sales of small quantities of black tin and copper ore up to 1879". The 70-inch engine house was blown up during World War II, for the same reason as those at Penhale Mine and Wheal Golden (see the note in Walk 5); the base of the house and the shaft can still be seen.

The main headland in front now is Cligga Head (Cornish "cleger": rocks, cliff). Notice the adits in the cliff below it. Soon the path passes through a big area where it seems the miners have left hardly a stone unturned. There are shafts very close to the cliff-edge in the section where the indentations are particularly dramatic. Collins says the Cligga area "has been a small tin-producer at intervals time out of mind". Several groups of ruined concrete buildings give evidence of quite recent industry: some date from World War II, when wolfram was mined here, others from the early 1960s, when Geevor Tin Mines Ltd sank a 200-foot shaft, and yet others may have been erected in the '70s, when further prospecting was done. The concrete buddles and other remains of dressing floors on the headland itself are of 1930s vintage. Just to the east of the headland there was a dynamite works, founded in 1889 as the British and Colonial Explosives Company and taken over in 1893 by the Nobel Explosives Company of Peace-Prize fame. It ceased manufacturing explosives in 1905 but was revived during World War I. At that time nearly a thousand people were employed, but the works closed almost as soon as hostilities ended. Details of the history and layout of the explosives works are given in Bryan Earl's "Cornish Explosives" (Trevithick Society, 1978), which includes a large-scale map and photographs. Bill Trembath tells of the watchman who guarded the nitroglycerine nitrator plant: his stool, it is said, had only one leg, so that if he should nod off he would have a rude and speedy awakening! After Cligga, the coastal footpath continues a little lower, near the cliff-edge. Now you are in the area worked by Great St George (otherwise known as Good Fortune), Wheal Perran, Wheal Leisure and Droskyn mines. Quite soon on your right, don't miss the entrance to an adit, one of the best examples in the area; it is easily accessible and can be explored if you have a torch - but please take great care. As you approach the headland at the west side of Perranporth beach (Droskyn Point), notice what Barry Atkinson calls "a particularly awesome man-made cavern, with passages leading off from it"; a fairly easy path leads down to it. **Continuing on the coastal footpath, eventually you will reach a kissing-gate by a road.**

❼ **Turn right, and then almost immediately left past the front of the "Droskyn Castle" hotel. If the tide is high you will have to return to the car park via the road** - notice the "caves" and arches in the small headland, most of which are in fact the work of countless miners over the centuries. **At low tide, however, it is well worth going round to the left and down steps to the rocks below.** A fair bit of scrambling is involved, but for those interested in the ancient mines it is worth the effort. There are innumerable adit-mouths, some a few feet up the cliff, and the whole headland is obviously honeycombed with shafts. Some man-made arches remain, others have collapsed, and the original shape of the cliffs has been entirely altered, as shown by the drawing on page 46, based on a photograph taken about 1850. Hamilton Jenkin writes: "In some places....workings were continued downward by means of shafts to a depth of 10 or 15 fathoms below sea level. To drain these, water was brought by a leat two miles up the Perran Coombe stream and thence through a tunnel, 700 ft. long, which was driven beneath the upper portion of the cliffs near the present Tywarnhayle Road." (Bill Trembath gives some details about the water channel, known as "Susan Tregay's Droke".) "From here," continues Jenkin, "the water descended through the most easterly shaft of the Old Droskyn Mine where it passed over a 22 ft. diameter pumping-wheel which was housed in an underground chamber hewn out of the solid rock. Beyond that the water flowed through a further tunnel, and over launders suspended across a cave, to another shaft, some 280 ft. to the west, where it drove another wheel of similar dimensions." It is only at exceptionally extreme spring tides that at low water you can walk round the small headland to the west and visit the magnificent caves known as Cathedral Caverns. Their old name was Vugah-en-Plunder, a hint of their value to smugglers or perhaps wreckers; it was, says Mr Trembath, the first Bishop of Truro who coined the more respectable name. Some dramatic mine workings are visible there, too, though it is said that one shaft was in fact made for the convenience of the smugglers. **To get back to your car you may prefer to return up the steps, but if you pick your way carefully it is possible to scramble around the rocks below the headland and get to the top by means of the wooden and stone stairs called Tamblyn Way; alternatively, you could wade across the stream and return to the car park across the beach.**

* * * * * * * * *

If, as I hope, doing walks such as this one has whetted your appetite for local history, I strongly recommend a visit to the excellent Perranzabuloe Folk Museum (*). It's not far from the main car park at Perranporth, and since there's very little parking space at the Museum it's best to walk there. To do so, go back to the bridge, turn left along the main street (St Piran's Road) and then left again at Porthmeor Road. You will soon come to the public library, on your right, and the museum is on the first floor of the same building. The Museum is normally open at Easter and then from 1st May till mid-September, Monday to Friday only, 10am to 1pm and 2-5pm.

PERRANZABULOE FOLK MUSEUM

The Museum opened in 1986, occupying premises which had originally been the Perranporth Oddfellows Hall and later belonged to a clothes manufacturer. At first the Museum shared the building with craft workshops, but these failed, and in 1989 the public library moved in to replace them. Though quite small, the Museum contains a wealth of fascinating material given or lent by local people, including some fine displays of mining photographs and artefacts. There is a model of St Piran's Oratory, and a full-scale replica of a Cornish cottage kitchen in late Victorian times.

PERRANPORTH INFORMATION CENTRE

This used to be in the same building as the museum, but now has much more spacious accommodation close to the main car park near the beach at the Seiners' Arms Hotel. Mrs Lawrence is a mine of general information about the Perranporth area and also holds a good stock of local maps and books - including Landfall Walks Books, of course! The normal opening hours are Monday to Friday 9.30-12.30 and 2.00-4.30, Saturday 9.30-12.30 only.

WALK 8

PORTHTOWAN, MINGOOSE & CHAPEL PORTH

About 6½ miles - shorter if you omit Tywarnhayle Mine

Here is another walk which takes in quite a tough section of the coastal path with fine cliff scenery and views. An "optional extra" on this walk is to explore the surface remains of Tywarnhale, a large and important copper mine with one of Cornwall's most dramatically situated inland engine houses. Like several other walks in this book, this one offers a strong contrast between the coastal and inland sections: as you wander along the pretty valley called "shady walk", or through the picturesque hamlet of Mingoose, it is almost incredible that those fearsome cliffs are hardly a mile away. Chapel Coombe is another very special place. There is little road walking. The path has sticky patches. There are toilets, shops and a pub at Porthtowan, and not far from the suggested route is the Victory Inn, which offers a varied and imaginative menu. The National Trust Beach Café at Chapel Porth (to quote my Gastronomy Correspondent, Gill Jacobs) "does wonderful food - garlic bread, croque monsieur and home-made ices!"

To drive to Porthtowan (*) from St Agnes, take the B3277 road towards Truro, turning sharp right after about a mile and a half, just before the Sevenmilestone garage. From the coast road above Porthtowan take the turning (again sharp right) down to the village and beach. Coming from Truro, take the A390 westwards; at the roundabout where this meets the A30 (Three Burrows or Chiverton roundabout) follow the sign to St Agnes, and after about two miles turn left just past the Sevenmilestone Garage. From there continue as described above. There are car parks on the right near the Porthtowan Inn (formerly called the Porpoise Inn) and by the beach.

PORTHTOWAN

A predecessor of mine, Victor Thursby, published in 1932 a little book called "Fourteen Hikes along the Cornish Coast", which is full of surprising observations. Perranporth, for example, he writes, "is delightfully situated in a picturesque valley." Well, I suppose you could argue that he had Perrancoombe in mind. But what of this sentence on the previous page? "Three miles from the start one comes to the quaint little village of Porth Towan, which strongly resembles Portreath." Had he actually been there? Or have sixty-odd years wrought even more dramatic changes to the Cornish landscape than I realised? "Quaint" is about the last adjective I'd have chosen for Porthtowan, and it would be quite low on the list for Portreath. There are, of course, a few substantial houses among the temporary-looking structures which have clustered around Porthtowan's fine beach, a favourite among surfers; one of the buildings, in fact, was a mine's engine house, as I have explained at the end of the directions. An interesting photograph on page 30 in Clive Benney's earlier volume shows a corn mill and attractive cottages close to where the Post Office now is, but that picture dates from 1904 - well before Mr Thursby's time. Although the name "Porthtowan" is recorded as far back as 1628, at that time there seem to have been only tin-stamps here: the village itself began to appear only 150 or 200 years later with the great growth of mines such as Wheal Towan and United Hills (Tywarnhayle). "Porthtowan" appears to mean "sand-dune cove". Sand, of course, is very much in evidence: in winter storms often carry it well up the road; but why the reference to sand-dunes, which would suit Perranporth far better? The answer may be, as Padel suggests, that the cove takes its name from Towan Farm, on the high ground a little to the east. So then one might ask why the farm is so called..... Similar doubts have been occasioned by the name of Pentewan (on the coast south of St Austell), which also has a Towan Farm nearby; Padel favours the theory that "towan" there refers to an old name for the nearby river.

❶ **To begin the walk, either go back up the road, turning left and right at the top, or to avoid what can be quite heavy traffic in summer use the footpath which runs behind the Porthtowan Inn and then to the left of bungalows, emerging at the coast road on the left side of Peter Johns' garage; you then turn right and immediately left.** You should now be walking inland, up the canyon-like valley with its rushing stream, and straight away on the left you will see the stack of an old mine building. This is a relic of the Echo Corner Shaft of South Wheal Towan (*).

SOUTH WHEAL TOWAN

This was a copper mine which sold ore to the value of nearly £118,000 between 1818 and 1847, but by 1870 was employing only eight people. Old photographs, such as the first one on page 30 in Clive Benney's earlier book, show twin stacks side by side here. A 40-inch pumping engine was installed, later to be replaced by a 70-inch. The cylinder bed stones from South Wheal Towan now belong to the museum at St Agnes, and are displayed outside. They are of special interest, because there are sets of bolt-holes for both the 40-inch and the 70-inch cylinders, suggesting that the engineers who installed the earlier engine anticipated the need for greater power later.

❷ Less than a hundred yards further on, go left up the rough and at times rather overgrown little path leading to a ruined engine house with a separate stack beside it - two of the surviving buildings from Tywarnhayle Mine (*). (Please note: this part of the walk is, strictly speaking, a diversion, and it involves some quite steep climbs, so you may prefer to continue up the road and follow the directions from point 3; but by doing so you will miss some of the most interesting and dramatically situated mining remains in Cornwall.)

TYWARNHAYLE MINE

For much of the information here and in the walk directions dealing with Tywarnhayle, I am indebted to an article in issue No. 4 of the St Agnes Museum Trust's Journal, by Dr Robin Smith of the Royal School of Mines. Tywarnhale, Tywarnhaile or Tywarnhayle ("ti war an hayle", house on the estuary) is really the name of an ancient manor, but is used to refer to a group of copper mines whose workings were combined. Wheal Rock was working at least as far back as 1750. In 1809 it was bought by Andrew Vivian, who re-named it United Hills. He installed a "little puffing engine" with a 12-inch cylinder, made by his partner, Richard Trevithick. After heavy losses, the mine was closed in 1815. A new company re-opened it in 1826, installing a 58-inch engine bought from Lambo Mine, Gwinear, and later an 80-inch, previously at Wheal Towan. This period witnessed two serious accidents, both caused by bursting boilers. The first, in 1827, caused no deaths but showered bricks and other debris into the valley. On Wednesday 3rd February 1830, nine people were killed, including a boy and a girl, when a boiler which had only recently been repaired at Redruth Hammer Mill exploded, completely without warning. Seven of the victims had been warming themselves before starting work. A ballad written at the time begins,

> 'Twas at Wheal Rock the boiler brok
> And eight poor men were killed
> And one poor maid...

The mine was at its most prosperous in the late 1830s; between 1836 and 1850, the depth of the workings increased from 36 to 100 fathoms below adit, and in the period 1826-52, 67,462 tons of copper ore were raised, according to the surviving records. Further losses led to closure in 1852. A new attempt was made in 1859, but despite the report in the "Western Daily Mercury" of 26 March 1864, *claiming that "there is little doubt that Tywarnhaile Mine will be one of the best copper mines in the country", this venture closed down later that same year (1864). In 1906 yet another company began work here, concentrating on the copper still remaining in the surface dumps and the underground workings above the water-line, which was at the 40-fathom level. They erected the Power House by the road, and used coal brought from Portreath to manufacture gas, which in turn powered generators to supply electricity to the new pump at Taylor's Shaft. This was the first electrically driven Centrifugal Pumping System used in Cornwall, and it worked very well; even so, the company, to quote Dr Smith, "went into liquidation" in 1907, and therefore the lower mine workings inevitably followed suit. H. V. Williams' little book and also the St Agnes Museum Trust's Journal No.4 have a photograph of the electric pump being lowered into place beside the already roofless engine house. The same picture is in Clive Benney's 1850-1920 book, plus another giving a more general view of Tywarnhayle at that period. At the same time, one of the first Elmore oil vacuum plants for flotation (separation of ore from unwanted material by forming a froth to which the ore particles cling) was installed; the remains of this can be seen below the small stack by Monkton's Shaft at the corner, opposite Wheal Music - point 4 in the directions. The inventor, Mr Elmore, was a director of the company at the time. Since 1908, apart from a period during World War II, Tywarnhayle has been in use to train mining students.*

The engine house, probably part of the old Wheal Rock, is thought to be one of the oldest surviving in the County. Its design is unique, and its engine, moved here some time after 1826, is said to have been the last one in Cornwall to use a wooden bob. Flat-rods were led from the bob kingpost through the rear window of the house to James' Shaft, on the higher ground. The trench is still visible on the hillside. **WARNING:** THE ENGINE HOUSE IS IN AN ADVANCED STATE OF DECAY, AND THE BOB WALL IN PARTICULAR LOOKS LIKE COLLAPSING QUITE SOON UNLESS STABILISING WORK IS CARRIED OUT. PLEASE HEED THE "DANGER" SIGN AND DO NOT ATTEMPT TO ENTER THE BUILDING. The bob wall overlooks an impressive shaft known as Taylor's, full of cavernous drippings and the sound of rushing water; it is covered with a metal cage, but care is still needed if you walk around the edge, because the ground is far from stable in places. Beside Taylor's Shaft are the foundations for the electric pump used here in 1906-7, and for an electric hoist. The buildings below, beside the road, include what was formerly the Power House for generating the electricity; they are used as a training centre by the Royal School of Mines, Imperial College, London. The School owns or leases all the workings of Tywarnhayle, and groups of mining students usually spend five weeks of their course here.

Return the same way, but just before reaching the road take the path almost straight ahead which climbs quite steeply. After a sharp right turn you pass a small quarry, probably the source of much of the stone in the older mine buildings, and soon afterwards you will see below you a long, low, ruined building which is said to have been the mine's Count House. On the left of the path as you approach the fine engine house at John's (or Roberts') Shaft on the top of the hill are the remains of sorting floors where stones of copper were hand picked from the mined rock, and spalling floors where workers used heavy hammers to break down large lumps. Above them, in an area now overgrown with gorse and bracken, was a pond to store cooling water for some of the mine's steam engines. From the engine house you have a good view of several shafts on the other side of the valley, each surrounded by the material extracted when it was sunk; these were all unsuccessful trial borings, made in hopes of finding a continuation of the lode. John's engine house contained a long-stroke 70-inch engine which later saw service at Wheal Uny, Redruth. (See "A View from Carn Brea", Walk 12.) Note the walled-in balance pit, which provided some shelter at this windy spot for the wooden balance bob. **Continue on the widish track leading towards a small building with a corrugated roof;** inside are benches and a hearth. This hut, used nowadays as a shelter by the students, stands by James' Shaft, which has a timber cover. **After passing the hut, take the track on the right,** and a few yards further on, just to the right of the track, is a little cutting leading to a mine portal; this was the access point for the pit railway. (Ore from the mine was hoisted to this point from the workings below, loaded into wagons, and taken by rail round the hill to dressing floors beside the road.) The gulley is rather overgrown, but you should have no great trouble walking along it. A timber framework prevents access to the shaft, but you can see quite far in and get some impression of underground workings. A little further on, beyond the boarded-up entrance to Gardiner's or Railway Shaft, the main track is blocked by a pile of rubble near Gardiner's Engine Shaft, where there was once an engine house for an 80-inch pumping engine, later replaced by a 70-inch one; the stack on the scree slope below belonged to a copper crusher which formerly stood beside the cottages below. By the track down there is the sewage farm, and further away, to the right, was the deep pit created by Wheal Music (*); when I researched this book originally in 1989 it was partially filled with sludge brought here from Wheal Concord (*), and by 1993 it had totally disappeared, the level surface of the infilling material now grassed over and looking like any other field. **Return from here to where the tracks divided, near the hut. The track bearing right leads back towards Porthtowan, so ignore this and turn left,**

returning by the same route past John's engine house and back down to the valley road.

WHEAL MUSIC

Despite its attractive name, in its early years Wheal Music had a grim reputation for serious accidents. The best-known relic of this mine was the "Navvy Pit". The copper here was mined down to about 300 feet, but at higher levels the lodes were, to quote George Henwood, "split up into minute strings and branches, none of which were singly worth pursuit. The whole rock was then removed and the copper ores extracted. An excavation of an elliptical form of about an acre in area and 25 fathoms in depth stands open to the day." (Henwood was writing in the middle of the 19th century.) All this openwork (or "stockwork") mining seems to have been done before 1833, and one early commentator stated that profits of £100,000 were made. During recent years the impressive cavity became a receptacle for rubbish, so the decision in the early 1980s to dump waste from Wheal Concord in it was regarded by many as an improvement, even though the obliteration of so notable a feature of the mining landscape is regrettable.

WHEAL CONCORD

In 1980 a company named Wheal Concord Ltd. was formed to explore for tin on the site of an old mine called Wheal Concord, west of Blackwater. By 1982, 21,000 tonnes had been raised by the workforce of forty, and some of its waste materials were dumped in the Navvy Pit. Because of problems over processing the operation ceased in 1982, but the workings were kept in viable condition, and in 1984 "development and exploration" was begun again by a different company. The sudden fall in tin prices in 1985 brought the operation to an end; the headgear is still in place at the shaft, but the chances of its ever being used again seem increasingly remote. The modern "Count House" at Blackwater became a restaurant but is now closed again.

❸ **Turn left on the valley road, passing the Power House and other former mine buildings.** Notice that the banks of the stream here are lined with walls; this is because the valley-floor level has been raised several feet by deposits of rubble from the mine. In the yard just past the buildings is a wooden trap-door; this is one route by which the students enter the shallower mine workings; the deeper ones are all flooded. The trap-door provides access to the Tywarnhayle adit, which flows under the road to join the stream, so the students have to wade.

❹ Just before the road bends right, notice on your left the ruins of the Elmore separation plant. **To continue the walk, turn left on to the track signposted to Tywarnhale Cottage;** but first it is worth going over to the right to inspect the engine house of Wheal Ellen (*), with its castellated stack. This never had an engine in it: it was built for a long-stroke Harvey 70-inch engine from Boscawen Mine (near Scorrier), but the cash ran out before it was moved and it ended up at a mine in mid-Wales! (The similarity of this building to the one which used to stand on the headland to the west side of Holywell - Wheal Golden - is mentioned in Walk 5.)

WHEAL ELLEN

This copper mine was also sometimes known as Old Basset Mine, not to be confused with the great Basset mines south of Carn Brea, although the name here, as there, presumably alludes to the great landowning family of Tehidy. Wheal Ellen worked mainly between 1826 and 1862, producing about 24,000 tons of copper ore. According to J.H.Collins, it "re-opened about 1907 for complex zinc-copper ores, but did not continue long." Some if not all of the concrete foundations and buildings near the engine house are relics of that period. Also nearby are much older structures - wheelpits and what look like calciners among them. Wheal Ellen is often spoken of as part of the Tywarnhayle group of mines, but in fact its workings were separate.

Like a small castle, Wheal Ellen guards
the entrance to the Porthtowan valley,
while the engine house at John's Shaft,
Tywarnhayle, stands sentinel above.

Now walk up the side-valley going north-east. Keep to the lower (right-hand) track. As is obvious because of all the old dumps and shafts on both sides of the stream, there were several small mines in this area, including Wheal Charles on the southern edge of Tywarnhayle; down beside the stream, Wheal Fancy and East Fancy, which produced tin; and Prince Royal further east, a copper mine. Wheal Fancy and Prince Royal were worked together under the name East Tywarnhayle by a company formed in 1864. After the sewage works, notice the shafts on the right. When I was last here, the slopes were a sea of brilliant yellow gorse. **Soon you have to cross the stream: there are a few rudimentary stepping stones, but some**

wading or a jump may be necessary after a wet spell. **The path continues by the stream along what the locals call "shady walk".** Certainly it is sheltered, if not often literally shady, and makes a delightful contrast to the exposed cliffs. As it is a bridleway, you may well encounter mud, but at the worst patch you can avoid it by walking on top of the bank to your left. A stone footbridge marks the start of a pretty footpath (not part of the route I am recommending here) which climbs through woodland to Trevissick Farm; from there the map shows it continuing to the road, but I haven't explored that end of it. Just before Banns Farm, flowing in from the right is water emerging from a small tunnel, an adit which appears to have belonged to a small mine called Wheal Banns, or possibly to Prince Royal Mine, mentioned above, or Trenethick Mine, another copper mine a little further east. According to Dines there are no records of output from Wheal Banns, but Collins mentions "small sales of tin ore about the year 1881". You are now coming into Banns Vale.

❺ At the road, turn left, and continue on the road for about half a mile. "Banns" means "hollow", and as you struggle up the hill on the far side you understand why the settlement is so called! Soon you have a good view of St Agnes Beacon ahead, with the engine houses of Wheal Coates on the skyline to its left; and much further left - almost behind you, in fact - is Carn Brea. **At the road, go straight across on to the track signposted to Mingoose and St Agnes. At the cottages (Trehane and Waterwheel Cottages), keep to the path on the right. Cross the stream by stepping-stones, and after the stile go diagonally to your right over the field: look for a stone stile. Cross this, and then keep near the hedge on your left; this should bring you to another stile and a road.**

❻ Turn left, and at the T-junction, by the attractively converted chapel, left again. You now pass through the pretty village of Mingoose (from the Cornish, "edge of the wood"). Near the valley-bottom is the former inn (the Miners Arms, which seems to have ceased business by 1880), and next to that Shasta Cottage, with its impressive granite lintels.

❼ A few yards later, take the public footpath on the right, signposted to Chapel Porth. (But if you're in need of refreshments, continue up to the main road - under half a mile - where you will find the Victory Inn.) **Keep to the main path down the valley.** After about half a mile, notice the evidence of mining on the far side of the valley. The hillside on the left, too, is riddled with shafts: at least ten are marked by warning posts all around the spoil heaps on the hilltop, and it is easy enough to walk through the low gorse and heather to see them.... but this is obviously the kind of area where wary walking is essential: please remember that old shafts whose existence has been forgotten sometimes suddenly reveal themselves in areas like this. As you continue along the main path near the stream you will see many more shafts on both sides. After you have passed the engine house of Charlotte United mine, built for a 30-inch pumping engine, **the path comes down close to the stream.**

❽ Take the wide track up the hillside to the left, which starts near the small (upper) footbridge.
(Alternatively, go down to the cove first. Refreshments are usually available at the National Trust car park in summer, and often even out of season. The site of the car park was once covered with mine buildings. A large waterwheel driving stamps once occupied the structure over-looking the toilets; the tailrace opening can still be seen, as well as the leat and dam further up the valley which supp-lied it. In the cliffs on the left are the mouths of two adits from Great Wheal Charlotte; on the right are two linked caves, known locally as "Two Vuggs". The right-

This drawing is based on a photograph taken in about 1912 of a small mine called Wheal Charlotte on the east side of Chapel Coombe. In the foreground are concave and convex buddles, and behind them is a battery of stamps driven by a small steam engine housed in the shed just left of centre.

hand one appears to have an adit opening at the far end, and the other has a "blow-hole": this is the hole associated in legend with the Giant Bolster.... See the note on St Agnes and its Church in Walk 9. If the tide is low enough - and, preferably, still going out - you may wish to walk along the beach on the right to explore the cave beneath Wheal Coates: see Walk 10. From the car park, you could cross the lower footbridge and go up the narrow path round the cliff-edge to continue the walk, if you have a good head for heights, or return up the valley and take the wide track I have mentioned.)
You are now on the coastal footpath, and don't need any further directions in order to find Porthtowan and your car. However, I should

point out that the large area of mine waste which you cross almost at once, as soon as you have passed the headland on the south of Chapel Porth, was created by Great Wheal Charlotte, and even though only the bob wall remains of its engine house, it is worth taking the path on the left to see it, looking now like a triumphal arch - or perhaps a monument to the memory of Cornish mining. The surviving records refer only to the period from 1834 to 1840, when just under 3,000 tons of copper were produced; but the records must be very incomplete, to judge by the devastation this mine caused along a large stretch of fine cliff. As you approach Porthtowan, you are in the area exploited by Wheal Towan (*), an important copper mine, but most of the evidence of its activities is further inland, near the road.

WHEAL TOWAN

A. K. Hamilton Jenkin tells in detail the story of Ralph Allen Daniell's faith in the prospects of this mine at the start of the 19th century. Eventually he was repaid with such handsome profits that he was nicknamed "Guinea-a-Minute Daniell". See the note on John Opie in Walk 7. The same nickname was given at about the same time to the owner of Wheal Neptune and other mines near Marazion: see "Mines and Miners of Cornwall" Vol. 4.

Beside the beach on the south side at Porthtowan, a dwelling, formerly a café, has been created from an old engine house: this was built in 1872 and belonged to New Wheal Towan, a small mine whose workings connected with those of Wheal Lushington, which was up on the cliff. Like the Wheal Ellen engine house, this building never had an engine in it. A rotative beam engine from Ireland was landed at Penryn and reached the site but was never erected. It was to have worked pumps underground by means of flat-rods going through the adit still visible behind. The bungalow next to New Wheal Towan engine house was originally of wood and was the former count house of Great Wheal Charlotte, taken down and re-erected as a dwelling. Bricks from the upper part of the engine house stack were used for the foundations.

NOTES

(1) Tywarnhayle Mine and Wheal Ellen are featured in "Exploring Cornish Mines", to be published soon by Landfall.
(2) A walk based on the area west of Porthtowan is included in "A View from Carn Brea".

WALK 9

IN AND AROUND ST AGNES VILLAGE

About 3 miles

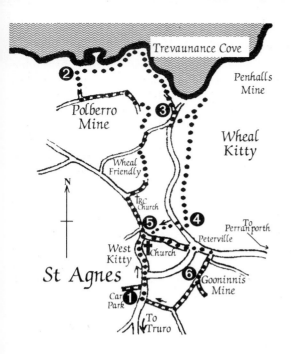

A short walk, but full of interest. Few Cornish villages are so dominated by the relics of mine buildings and yet so attractive. The walk visits or passes very close to five imposing engine houses, plus dozens of other associated buildings and workings, some of the latter being extremely ancient. You will also see what little remains of the harbour built to serve the mines. There are two quite steep climbs. It should be reasonably dry underfoot all the way. St Agnes has toilets, pubs and shops; there is also a pub near the beach at Trevaunance, and two cafés open in the season.

This walk starts at St Agnes car park, Trelawny Road. For instructions on driving there from Truro, see Walk 10.

❶ **Return to the main street and turn left.** (For information about the West Kitty Thomas' Shaft engine house, close to the car park, see Walk 10.) **Continue through the centre of St Agnes (*) and turn left on to Trevaunance Road, which is just past the parish church.** On the right a short way along Trevaunance Road is Castle House. According to Maurice Bizley it was once an inn, and there are traditions that it acted as a refuge during the Civil War for either Prince Charles or his brother James, and that a tunnel links it to the Vicarage garden next door. Prospect House, on the left roughly opposite, is the former count house of West Kitty mine. Just behind it is Reynold's Shaft, where there was a 50-inch pumping engine. The engine house was demolished some twelve or fifteen years ago to make way for housing.

ST AGNES AND ITS CHURCH

There has been a church here since at least the 14th century, but little apart from the base of the tower remains of any old building, although some of its stone was used when it was rebuilt on a larger scale in 1848 by J.P.St Aubyn, the highly industrious Victorian architect who has left his mark on almost every old church in the County. As with so many other Cornish mining communities, this was a period of great expansion in population. The highest census figure for the population of St Agnes was 7,757, in 1841. A market house used to stand where the lych gate is now, but was demolished in 1894 so that the road could be widened. Clive Benney in his earlier volume tells the story of the "fireball" which struck the spire at St Agnes in 1905; and in 1929 lightning again struck: "the top of the spire, weighing over half a ton, was hurled eastwards about ten feet and fell, after smashing the roof, in one solid mass. Not a stone of it was loosened by the fall and it was later placed outside the south porch of the church." (Quoted from "A Portrait of a Village Church", the very detailed and interesting booklet available in the church.) Granite blocks from the destroyed harbour were used to build the high altar. St Agnes was a Roman martyr of the 4th century; whether she had any connection at all with this village or this church is very doubtful, although several local legends exist which refer to her, notably the one telling how she was wooed by the giant Bolster, who could step in one stride from St Agnes Beacon to Carn Brea. The red stain on the side of a hole above the sea at Chapel Porth was, it is said, caused when she tricked him into spilling his own blood down it: only on that condition would she be his bride. For the likely origin of the name Bolster, see the note on St Agnes Beacon, Walk 10. It has sometimes been stated that the original dedication of the church was to St Ann, who had Irish connections, like most of the other saints of North Cornwall, but no written evidence exists of such a dedication; more likely, "Ann" is merely a dialect form of "Agnes". A discredited suggestion is that "St Ann" was a misunderstanding of the Celtic phrase, "San Tan", meaning "Sacred Fire"; quite what sacred fire has to do with this place I don't know. Most of the older guide books state that the local people refer to the village as "St Ann's". An old name for it was "Bryanek", with many variant spellings. Thomas Tonkin, back in about 1720, had suggested that this meant "the Village under the Hill", but later changed his mind and decided on "a Place Where Rushes Grow, for such it was within the memory of man, before the adits drained it." John King tentatively explains the old name as "Town of Spar Stone or burying place," and Nicholas Johnson offers "peaked hill, prominent hill" ("Cornish Archaeology", 1980). Oliver Padel, the leading authority on Cornish place-names, is unable to explain the name beyond translating the first syllable as "hill". Just in case you're not sufficiently confused already by this plethora of possible meanings, Ann Preston-Jones has put forward the attractive theory that "St Agnes" may have originated as "Stênes", meaning "place of tin".

Immediately after the Roman Catholic Church, consecrated in 1958, turn right on a track which soon brings you to the splendid engine house and other old buildings of Wheal Friendly (*), spectacularly situated with Trevaunance Cove as a backdrop, and the buildings of Wheal Kitty and Polberro Mine dominating the skyline to the east and west respectively.

Wheal Kitty, on the far side of the valley, glimpsed from Wheal Friendly

WHEAL FRIENDLY

Although not a very success-ful mine, if the surviving records are a fair indication (only 450 tons of copper and about the same amount of tin over a period of some fifty years), quite a lot of its buildings and other relics such as leats have survived in good condition. Wheal Friendly was linked with West Kitty mine. Roger Radcliffe has passed on to me what he was told by the late Bill Harper, who used to live on the site of the old West Kitty Mine. His father worked at Wheal Friendly. It was such a wet mine that on one occasion when the pumping engine had stopped for some reason there was a very rapid inflow of water in the deep part where he was working. He hurried away from his place of work and had to swim the last few feet to the ladderway by the time he arrived at the shaft. The mine's name means "rich" or "profitable": compare all the mines named "Wheal Prosper". Such names were, no doubt, intended to encourage adventurers to provide the necessary investment.

Continue down the narrow path which starts beside the entrance to a walled yard - in fact this was once the mine's water reservoir; water for it was pumped from the mine and ducted in from West Kitty across the fields. The path next passes the remains of one wall of another engine house. This was for a horizontal whim and/or pneumatic stamps engine. **After a few steps, the path goes left, towards Polberro, and descends into a little valley** which was once the deer park belonging to the Tonkin family of Trevaunance Manor - more about them later. The site of the manor house is a little way up to the left. **At the road, Rocky Lane, turn right, and then almost immediately left.** There used to be a public footpath sign to The Cliffs here, but now (early 1994) only the post it was once attached to remains. **You pass beside a metal gate to the right of the entrances to Little Orchard Village. After a row of fir trees on your left, the path continues ahead, quite steeply uphill.** Soon you will see evidence of old mining all around, in the form of capped shafts and the disturbed ground left by open-cast workings. **When you reach the wider track at the top, turn right and continue until you reach an old chimney stack,** part of Polberro Mine (*); look left for a good view of the Turnavore Shaft engine-house, with its corrugated-asbestos roof. (Beside it are large concrete dressing floors with several convex buddles, shown in my drawing. Unfortunately, the track leading past these to the engine house is private. A similar area of dressing floors is to be seen at Wheal Kitty, later on this walk; in fact, the dressing floors at Polberro were transferred from Wheal Kitty in about 1937.) **Just before the stack, turn right on to a track that leads down to the cliff edge.** The stack belonged to an arsenic burning house, and was originally taller, with a brick top section. The lack of any remains of a "lambreth" flue suggests that no attempt was made to collect the arsenic.

The Turnavore engine house, Polberro Mine.
Dressing floors with convex buddles in the foreground.

An extract from an advertisement in the "West Briton".
See the note on Polberro Mine overleaf.

Valuable TIN MINES called the ROYAL POLBEROU CONSOLS, in the parish of St Agnes, within eight miles of Truro, Cornwall, with the Engines, Machinery and Materials thereon.

To be SOLD .... in ONE LOT, at the PUBLIC SALE ROOMS .... at Gray's Inn Coffee House, Holborn, London, on FRIDAY, the 31st day of March next, at Twelve o'clock at Noon, all those extensive and valuable TIN MINES well known as the **ROYAL POLBEROU CONSOLS MINES,** .... which have for many years past averaged the monthly produce of 30 tons of Black Tin of excellent quality. These mines extend under a surface of upwards of 200 acres, and contain 24 shafts, 9 of which are now in full working, with about 3,000 fathoms of levels, and are held under grants or setts, of which 13 years and upwards are unexpired, at the very moderate dues of 1-20th, TOGETHER WITH THE STEAM ENGINES, MACHINERY, ERECTIONS, BUILDINGS, AND OTHER MINING EFFECTS therein belonging, comprising TWO STEAM PUMPING ENGINES of 60 inches cylinder each, five Boilers, Balance Bobs, &c. complete; TWO STEAM WHIMS, respectively 22 and 20 inches cylinder, with 4 Boilers, to one of which is attached a Crusher; a 30 inches cylinder Steam Stamping Engine, with 3 Boilers; 64 Heads Frames, Passes, Pits, &c., complete; 2 sixteen Heads Stamping Mills, with 2 wheels, each 30 feet in diameter, and 3 feet abreast, with Lifters, Passes, &c., complete; every requisite for dressing and calcining Tin, and a Sawing Machine and Water Wheel. The Buildings comprise Sump Men's and Changing Houses, Smiths' and Carpenters' Shops, Counting, Store, Captains, Gig, Engineers, Stamping, Casting, Tin Dressers, and Changing Houses, the latter with 193 Miners' chests;

also, Assay Office, with every requisite; 2 Stables, 1 Powder Magazine, 1 covered Sawpit, with frames. The Smiths' Shop, which has every convenience for 5 forges, with powerful Punching and Screw Machines, Kibble-mould, and Tools of every description. A large Machine, Turning Lathe, and other requisites in the Engineer's House. Also, all the Pitwork Ladders, Casings, Brass Air Pump, 10 Horse Whims, Sheaves, Kibbles, and Drawing and Tramming Carriages and Apparatus; Weighing House, Beams, Scales, and Weights; Counting House and other Furniture; 3 Dials, 2 Crab Winches, Large Steelyard, 150 Barrows, Capstans and Shears, Capstan and other Ropes, Flat Rod and Stands, Rods, Clack-seat Pieces, Pumps, H and Top Door Pieces, Working Barrels, Plunger Poles, Stuffing Boxes and Glands, Rod Plates, Common Plates, Staples and Glands, Block Pins, Rod Pins, Connexion Rods, Blocks, Cisterns, nearly 2,000 fathoms of Wood and Iron Tram Roads, with all the Leavings, Halvans, Barrows, and other Property and Effects of the Mine (except the Stores and other Articles hereinafter mentioned to be taken at a valuation).

The Store Yards, &c., contain large quantities of Iron, Boiler, and Kibble Plates, Candles, Gunpowder, Hilts, Leather, Tallow, Grease, old Copper and Lead, about 4,000 lbs of old Brass, 2 Horses, Gig and Harness, 3 Carts and Harnesses, Debenture and other Timber, Coals, Rope, &c., and other Materials of daily consumption; which, with the Tin Stuff and Tin Ores on the Mines at the time of completing the Sale, are to be taken at a fair valuation by the purchaser.

The outlay on this property has been upwards of £100,000, and the Setts, which are very large and extensive, are now in full working, and are well found in every respect.

Dated February 24, 1843

WALK 9

POLBERRO MINE

Peter Stanier states that Polberro was "once the richest mine in Cornwall". This mining area is certainly one of the most ancient and intensively worked in Cornwall, and doubtless gave rise to the old Cornish saying, "Stean San Agnes an guella stean en Kernow", "St Agnes tin is the finest tin in Cornwall." According to R. H. Bird, the mine was renamed "Polberro Royal Consols" after a visit by Queen Victoria in 1846; but when it was advertised for sale in "The West Briton" in 1843 it was already called "Royal Polberou Consols". One explanation I have come across is that it had produced silver for the Royal Mint. The advert, part of which I have typed out for this book, gives some idea of the range of equipment and buildings used by a fair-sized mine. It also shows how colourful much of the technical terminology was. Polberro's main period of activity was from 1837 to 1895, and the surviving engine house was built in 1887 for a 60-inch engine which had previously been at South Penstruthal Mine (Lanner) and before that at North Pool. From Polberro the engine made one more move, a short one this time to Wheal Friendly. The Turnavore Shaft was re-opened from 1937 to 1941 and deepened to over a thousand feet. The plant at that time was all electrical, and the old engine house was roofed to provide a changing-house for the miners. (The name, by the way, comes from the same Cornish originals as Polperro and Polperrow - a farm near Tresillian - and seems to mean "Peter's pool" or "Pyra's pool".)

❷ **Turn right on the coast path.** The cliff scenery is splendid here - but notice too, on your right, all the debris and capped shafts, the remains of very ancient mining. Before long, as you approach a headland, you will see a concrete leat leading to the cliff edge. This originally ran from the dressing floors at Turnavore, Polberro. If you walk (carefully!) to the far end of it and look at the cliff face to your left, you will see the mouth of an adit from Polberro about half way up the cliff. A little lower down the path, just before the main flight of steps, there is another adit portal on your right. Near the foot of the steps are the remains of storage "hutches" - rather similar to the eight hutches at Devoran Quay: see "A Second View from Carn Marth", Walk 11 - which are now the clearest evidence that St Agnes once had a harbour (*); a little later, just after you have passed the Trevaunance Cove Hotel, if you look down to the beach you will see a scattering of large granite blocks, all that now remains of the last harbour. Before that, while you are still near the hutches, look inland to see an upper section of the concrete leat or aqueduct from Turnavore, and below it a fine example of "old men's workings". The cave is wholly man-made, part of the excavations of an old mine called Wheal Luna.

ST AGNES HARBOUR

As the centre of a busy mining district at a time when inland transport varied from difficult to impossible, St Agnes urgently needed a harbour, and from 1632 onwards at least five attempts were made to build one, but sea storms always won in the end. The one which lasted easily the longest was built in 1793 at a cost, according to Murray's Handbook for Devon and Cornwall (1859), of £10,000; it survived intact till 1915, but during that summer one stone in the North Quay was washed away; the damage was not repaired, and an autumn gale breached the wall. By 1924, the once impressive harbour was reduced to a heap of stones. Several photographs exist, however (one of which was the basis for the drawing here), showing the two quays protecting a space big enough for about six coasting ships. Apart from a narrow flight of steps and a ladderway, there was no access to the quays from inland. Ore from the storage hutches was loaded on to the vessels by two long chutes, and incoming cargoes had to be lifted in baskets or "kibbles" attached to ropes which passed over pulleys on a wooden platform built out over the cliff edge. These were operated by two horsewhims about thirty feet from the edge. The principal uses of the harbour were for the shipping out of copper ore for smelting in South Wales and the import of coal for the mine engines, but it also allowed a pilchard fishery to be established. The bulk of the St Agnes Museum Trust's Journal No.6 (1990) is devoted to studies of the harbour and its history by Roger Radcliffe and Ann Preston-Jones. The scale model of St Agnes harbour at the local museum is excellent, and gives a clearer impression than words or even maps and photographs can of how it was designed and operated.

Continue along the wide track, past the Trevaunance Point Hotel, and after the public toilets (closed in winter) you will come to a road close to the beach. It is worth going down to the beach to see the mouth of the main Polberro adit gushing water on the left. (An interesting old photograph of this adit is included in "Bygone Cornwall" - details at the end of the directions for Walk 5 - showing the large group of mine buildings at Wheal Friendly in the background and a tin recovery plant building overshadowing the beach.) The cliff on the right is dominated by the spoil heaps of Penhalls Mine and Wheal Kitty, and less than half-way up the cliff-face below them is another adit-mouth.

❸ Walk up the road, and turn left on to the coast path just before you reach the Driftwood Spars Hotel. (During the 19th century this building was used as a store for the mines and other industries in the valley, which included a hammer mill and a small iron foundry.) The climb is quite stiff, and you may well be glad of the seat at the top; from here you have a fine view of the site of the harbour, as well as Wheal Friendly and Polberro. To inspect the surface remains of Wheal Kitty (*), take the path on the right - not the one signposted to St Agnes, but the rougher track heading towards the engine house.

Soon you reach extensive concrete dressing floors, with several good examples of convex buddles. The engine house on Sara's Shaft was, when "A View from St Agnes Beacon" was written, surrounded by buildings dating from the late 1920s, when this mine was last worked; many of those buildings have since been demolished.

Early 20th century dressing floors at Wheal Kitty Wheal Friendly and Polberro on the skyline.

WHEAL KITTY

This was one of the most important of St Agnes' mines, producing, according to the surviving records, 13,121 tons of tin and 2,024 tons of copper between 1834 and 1930. Like nearly all these enterprises, it was an amalgamation of many smaller mines, some very ancient. The Sara's Shaft house contained a 65-inch pumping engine. In 1905 the stamps engine house, which stood among the older dressing floors a little to the south-west of Sara's Shaft, was burnt down, probably as a result of arson by a sacked official. The engine itself and part of the bob wall survived, and the old photograph reproduced in my drawing gives some idea of how a beam engine was used to provide rotative power. In J.H.Collins's book, whose statistics I have quoted so often, it is amusing to see how, writing in 1912, he advertises the recent successes of Wheal Kitty, which his own company had purchased soon after the fire. His new enterprise amalgamated Penhalls and Gooninnis Mines with the original Wheal Kitty.

(For a much more detailed study of the surface remains of Wheal Kitty and Penhalls Mine, see "Exploring Cornish Mines", soon to be published by Landfall.)

After the fire at Wheal Kitty, 1905. The base of the stamps engine house still stands among the undergrowth on the slopes of Trevaunance Coombe.

Return to the coast path and take the inland path signposted to St Agnes, which provides you with fine views over Trevaunance Coombe. Photograph 89 in J. Trounson's book makes an interesting comparison with the scene today. One of the most notable sons of St Agnes parish was the historian Thomas Tonkin (1678-1742); he was born at Trevaunance Manor, on the other side of the valley, and it was his family who had pioneered early attempts to build a harbour at Trevaunance Porth. The clatter of machinery must have dominated life in the Coombe in his day, for he writes, "The water arising on Trevaunance, in conjunction with Breanick (St Agnes) water-course, drives twelve stamping mills, and a griest mill ...." and he adds, "There was formerly in Trevaunance Coom a blowing house with anothor griest mill ..." A century or more after his death there were a hammer mill and an iron foundry in the valley.

The path eventually descends to the road.

❹ Turn right, and after a few yards take the path on the left, signed to the Glen Hotel. This takes you up beside the much-photographed row of cottages called Stippy Stappy. Older names were Bosun's Row or simply Cottage Row.

❺ At the road, you could turn right to return directly to the car park, but if you are not already tired of looking at old mines, turn left and walk down to Peterville - an area which in the days before motorised traffic provided a useful open space for village events. It was once graced with the name "Dirtypool". Dirtypool Forge, which then stood opposite what is now the Peterville Inn, and the Dirty Pool Malting Co., which formerly supplied malt for brewing to those eight pubs, perhaps created much of the dirt. At various times there were also a cobbler, a wheelwright and a carpenter. One of the photographs in Clive Benney's earlier volume shows Peterville in about 1905, with a coalyard on one side and the Reynold's Shaft engine house of West Kitty, complete with headgear, towering above. **Just beyond the pub** ("The Victoria" in Dirtypool days), **take the second turning on the right, signposted to Goonown and Goonbell.**

❻ After passing the Rosevean Hotel, fork left up a small side road leading to the Mount Pleasant nursing home. The farm track on the left at the top leads to the remains of Gooninnis Mine (*), which suffered damage during the winter of 1992-3, when lightning struck the engine-house stack. The buildings are on private land, but the owner, Mr Roy Blewett, tells me he has no objections to visitors inspecting them, so long as they do not tamper with farm or stable equipment, and securely fasten the gate on leaving.

GOONINNIS MINE

The remains of this mine, with its two castellated stacks, are all the more impressive in view of the fact that Gooninnis (often spelt Gooninis) was only a trial working in search of tin. It started in 1873 but was most active between 1899 and 1907. The 50-inch pumping engine, after several years at Trevaunance Mine (Walk 10), was operating here by 1901 and removed in 1910. No record exists of any actual output; its lodes were linked to those of Wheal Kitty, and its returns were included in those of the larger mine. In an area as intensively mined as this, workings inevitably overlapped: apparently West Kitty, Wheal Kitty and Blue Hills - see Walk 7 - all interconnected underground. If you can get hold of the St Agnes - Perranporth volume of A. K. Hamilton Jenkin's "Mines and Miners of Cornwall", now out of print, look at the map on page 29, dating from 1838, which shows the complex pattern of setts in this area. The harbour and hutches at

Trevaunance Cove are also shown. Clive Benney's 1850-1920 volume includes interesting photographs showing Gooninnis; one of them illustrates well how massive the steam-engine bobs (beams) were. It shows the bob being removed to Castle an Dinas, near St Columb Major, in 1911; the engine, with a new bob, still survives at Goonvean Clay Pit. (The name, Gooninnis, is also that of a nearby farm; it probably means "isolated, remote spot on the down": "innis" seems to derive from enys or ynys, literally an island. Goon, meaning "down" or "rough grazing land" is a common element in place-names around St Agnes: Goonbell, "distant downs", Goonvrea, "hilly pasture", and Goonlaze, "green down", are some. "Goonvean" means "small downland.")

Return to the road at the bottom, turn left, and then take the first right turning, passing the Rosemundy House Hotel. "Rosemundy" is a name that reflects the importance of mining in the story of St Agnes: *ros mon-dy,* "moorland mineral house", by which I suppose is meant an ore-bin. **This road brings you to the main street opposite the Railway Inn (*); here turn right, and for the car park turn left.**

THE RAILWAY INN

This dates back to the 17th century, and was originally called The Smith's Arms, because there was a smithy behind it. A shaft of an old mine called Polbreen is also behind the inn, and there is a legend that the workings nearby are haunted by the ghost of Dorcas, a girl who committed suicide by jumping into the shaft after her fiancé died in a mining accident. The story also tells how the ghost once saved a young miner underground by calling him away from a spot where the roof was just about to cave in. "At certain times," writes Frank Pearce in an old St Agnes guide book (from which I have taken all the above information about the inn), "the sound of the sea can still be heard through the tunnels under 'The Railway'." In 1904, when the railway line reached St Agnes, the name was altered to The Smith's Arms and Railway Hotel. The inn was not, in fact, very close to the railway, which ran nearly a mile south of the village, and crossed the main road towards Truro on a bridge whose remains are still a prominent landmark; the station was near the bridge, at Great Western Railway Yard, and its main building is still easily recognisable, converted for use as industrial units; there was also a halt at Goonbell. (The diesel shunter engine on display beside St Agnes station probably dates from the 1960s. It had previously been bought by someone at Goonhavern who had plans to develop part of the old railway line there as a tourist attraction.) The line from near Chacewater to Perranporth was opened in 1903, and two years later it reached Newquay. Although it was well-used by holidaymakers, it was "axed" by Dr Beeching in 1963. Its track would have made a fine footpath, but it was sold off piecemeal, and much of it is now covered with rubbish or gorse and brambles.

ST AGNES MUSEUM

Before you leave St Agnes, if you are at all interested in industrial archaeology and local history - and I don't think you would be reading this book otherwise - you should make a point of visiting the museum. It occupies a former chapel at the village cemetery, which is on the left as you enter St Agnes from the south, just before the turning to Chapel Porth, and only 250 yards from the main car park. Opening hours are from 10.30 a.m. to 5 p.m. every day including Sundays from 1st April to the end of September (possibly a little later in 1994). Among many other displays, it features local minerals and mining, and has an interesting video about the tin streaming still being practised at Blue Hills: see Walk 7. There is a most impressive model of the old harbour. The Trust has published eight annual journals, and a ninth is due out in 1994, price £1.75. They contain many fascinating articles, often of special interest to the "industrial archaeologist".

ST AGNES LEISURE PARK

Not far beyond the Museum's new premises is the Leisure Park, which features, among beautiful gardens, a famous collection of scale models. Some of them would, I feel, be of special interest to readers of this book, especially the Old Cornish Mining Village, which includes the Miners Arms at Mithian (Walk 7); and above all the working model of the surface buildings of a typical Cornish tin mine, complete with pumping and whim engine houses, crusher, stamps, settling tanks and arsenic calciner.

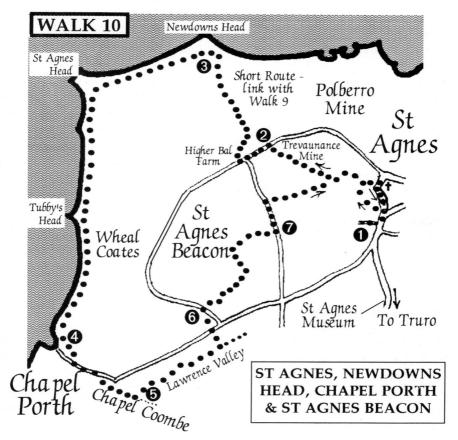

Newdowns Head

St Agnes
Head

Short Route -
link with
Walk 9

Polberro
Mine

St
Agnes

Higher Bal
Farm

Trevaunance
Mine

Tubby's
Head

Wheal
Coates

St
Agnes
Beacon

St Agnes
Museum

To Truro

Chapel
Porth

Lawrence Valley

Chapel Coombe

**ST AGNES, NEWDOWNS
HEAD, CHAPEL PORTH
& ST AGNES BEACON**

*About 6 miles. An alternative route of
about half that length is also suggested.*

There are few Cornish headlands more spectacular than St Agnes Head, few
mine buildings more wonderfully situated than Wheal Coates. Chapel
Coombe is well worth a second visit, and the little valley that follows it on
the walk is one of those charmed spots that nestle among hillsides bare but
for the ever-glowing gorse. Finally there is "a view from St Agnes Beacon",
which made an even more appropriate conclusion for this book under its
earlier title than it does now!

You will probably need waterproof footwear for that valley; elsewhere you
are mostly on well-made tracks, with just a few yards on roads. Except in St
Agnes, there are no shops or pubs on the route, but toilets and café are open
in the season at Chapel Porth. The Victory Inn is not very far from point 5
on the map: see Walk 8.

WALK 10

The walk starts at St Agnes. To drive there from Truro, take the A390 westwards to the Chiverton Cross roundabout and follow the St Agnes sign from there. The car park is on Trelawny Road, to the left just after you enter the main street.

❶ From the car park, return to the main street and turn left. Notice the Miners' and Mechanics' Institute (*) on the left.

ST AGNES MINERS' & MECHANICS' INSTITUTE

Above the date, 1893, are the initials JPE. John Passmore Edwards is a name you will see on many public buildings, especially libraries, in Cornwall; he also established hospitals, art galleries, technical schools and colleges, including some in London, and endowed an English scholarship at Oxford. He was born nearby at Blackwater in 1823, the son of a carpenter, and began by selling strawberries when his father turned to market gardening. Later he became involved in journalism in London, and after several loss-making ventures he made a success of "Building News", and later bought the "Echo", the first halfpenny newspaper. He was a well-known champion of causes such as Early Closing and Anti-Gambling, and as a pacifist he denounced the Crimean and Boer Wars. He was Liberal MP for Salisbury from 1880 to 1885, and died in 1911. He twice refused a knighthood. He once offered to build a lighthouse on St Agnes Beacon, but the authorities (The Trinity Brethren) did not feel that one was required there; they also said that if it was erected the light would be so high that it would be sometimes lost in the mists. When Edwards laid the foundation stone at the St Agnes Institute, a "time capsule" containing coins, newspapers and a programme of the day's events was placed beneath it; Clive Benney in his earlier volume tells how it was stolen a few days later and afterwards replaced with a new one. (In 1993 the St Agnes Museum Trust published a booklet about John Passmore Edwards and the Institute in celebration of its centenary.)

Soon after this, turn left opposite Pengarth Road to get a good view of the Thomas' Shaft pumping-engine house and nearby stack - parts of West Kitty mine (*).

WEST KITTY

This mine in the centre of St Agnes began in 1863 and worked until 1916. It produced a little copper, but mainly tin ore, which was taken to the stamps at Jericho (Walk 7) for crushing. West Kitty was formed from several older mines, in one of which the mineral called stannite, tin pyrites or bell-metal ore was discovered in about 1785; this is much rarer than the usual tin-bearing ore, cassiterite. The discoverer was a German, Rudolf Erich Raspe, best known as the author of the fantastic stories of the travels of Baron Munchausen, which he wrote when he was storekeeper at Dolcoath Mine, Camborne. The original steam engine which pumped water from the Thomas section of West Kitty was later employed at Carpalla china clay works and is still preserved - though in bits and unrestored - in a store at the Science Museum, South Kensington. The Thomas Shaft engine house was repaired and made safe by Carrick District Council in 1990.

Turn right at the T-junction, go along the path and road into the council estate, turn right at the next T-junction, bear right into Beaconsfield Place, and then left at the old cottage on the left, Bramble Cottage. When you come to a stile ahead, don't cross it but turn right and walk between hedges. Now you come to another stile; cross that, and then head just left of the stack to a further stile at the field corner. After a rather muddy stretch you cross another stile; keep heading slightly left of the stack to cross yet another stile, and then turn right, passing the chimney. This and the ivy-covered ruined buildings nearby are parts of Trevaunance Mine (*). **Continue to the road.**

TREVAUNANCE MINE

Known at various times as Wheal Trevaunance and Trevaunance Consols or Trevaunance United (when it joined forces with Goonlaze Mine), this was "a very ancient and profitable mine, said to have given £100,000 in dividends" (Collins). Both tin and copper were produced, and it worked continuously for 150 years. An interesting article by Roger Radcliffe in the first Journal of the St Agnes Museum Trust focuses on the early history of Wheal Trevaunance. Just how old the mine is is uncertain, but the neighbouring Pell Mine was active as early as 1511, and there are records of the driving of adits by Wheal Trevaunance in the 1720s and 1775. Mr Radcliffe illustrates his claim that in the latter part of the 19th century Trevaunance was "perhaps the most primitive mine in the county" by the fact that steam power did not reach it till the 1880s; until then, any workings below adit were, it seems, drained "by means of barrels hauled by windlass, or later by horse whim" and perhaps also by hand pumps. The big beam engines were commonly moved from site to site according to demand, and the Gooninnis engine (see Walk 9) worked here between 1884 and 1900. The low building is the remains of the whim engine house; the engine was completely enclosed, like the recently restored one at Levant (see "A View from Carn Galver", Walk 4), and came from Wheal Coates nearby. H.G.Ordish's 1967 volume has a photograph of the engine houses as they were in 1935. The stack of the 50-inch pumping engine house remains, but the rest of the building was pronounced unsafe and demolished in 1984. The St Agnes Museum Trust secured the preservation of what you now see.

❷ **Turn left and continue along the road as far as the left turning to The Beacon and Mingoose. Here take the track on the right, beside Higher Bal Farm (*).**

BAL

Bal or Ball is a Cornish word for a working place, especially a group of mines; usually mines called Bal are older than those named Wheal. A.K.H.Jenkin mentions fifteen small ancient mines in this area which were later combined into the workings of Polberro. Trevaunance Bal was divided into as many as eighty tin bounds, Wheal Pasty among them. A vivid impression of the vast number of small old mines around St Agnes is given in "Friendly Retreat"; their names include Wheal Madly, Great Wheal an Cracke, Space Bean, Wheal Drunkard and Great Dribble.

At the small chapel, now a house, bear right. Ignore the first track on the left; keep to the main one, which bends left and passes a bungalow called West Polberro; ignore the left turning, to New Downs Farm, and follow the track round to the right till you reach a road. Here turn left. When you reach the sign of Bawden Manor Farm, take the grassy track on the right. The seat here makes a good opportunity for a picnic stop: the view in clear conditions extends along the coast past Cligga Head, Perran Sands, Ligger and Penhale Points to the lighthouse at Trevose. Inland can be seen the tall windmills at Carland Cross; and you may well have the gliders from Trevellas airfield to entertain you. **The path soon brings you down to the coastal footpath.**

❸ **For the shorter walk turn right on the coast path.** The first section of it is dominated by the old workings of Polberro Mine. **After about half a mile, when you see a mine stack quite close, up on your right, pick up the directions given for Walk 9 at point 2. At point 3, to take the most direct route you could keep on up the road instead of continuing on the coast path, turning right on the path to the Glen Hotel and Stippy Stappy, as described in point 4.**

For the full walk to Chapel Porth and the Beacon, turn left on the coast path, passing the National Trust sign, Newdowns Head. From here if you look back you will see two capped mineshafts, and indeed almost everywhere along this part of the coast there is evidence of mining, particularly as you approach St Agnes Head. **Follow the acorn signs.** Just as you are about to reach the Head there is a small quarry on the left where drilled holes can be seen in the rock face. Soon after the Head, where a wall starts on the left, there is a deep capped shaft by the cliff edge, with a cobbled area beside it whose purpose I can only guess at. This was probably part of Wheal Bungay, a mine which Collins lists but gives no information on. The famous and highly photogenic clifftop buildings of Wheal Coates (*) now come into view. As you approach them, it is worth following the rough little paths to the left to visit the small stack over there, because this gives you a clear view of the vast amount of openwork mining that took place here before the shafts were sunk.

Continue to the upper group of mine buildings, which include the restored, three-storeyed stamps engine house with the smaller building behind it that housed the whim, and behind that the more modern horizontal whim.   Just south of the buildings is a well-preserved mine pond, and on the seaward side are the remains of dressing floors, including a ruined burning house or calciner. The sturdy chimney stack at the top - originally much taller - served that as well as the boiler house for the stamps and whim engines.   Best-known of all is the restored 30-inch pumping engine house below at Towanroath Shaft.   Beside that stands its boiler house, which was modified in 1910 to house a steam pump. ("Towanroath", sometimes spelt "Towanwroath", is the name of the cave below. It means "the hole, or perhaps hollow place, of the hag or witch".)

Towanwroath Vugga, with the 30-inch
pumping-engine house on Towanroath
Shaft, Wheal Coates, above.

WHEAL COATES

Wheal Coates was already described as "old" in 1720, but most of the earliest workings must have been by means of gunnises in Towanwroath Vugga (cave) and the cliff face, together with shallow pits and trenches following the lodes inland. By 1828 the mine had acquired a steam engine. During the 1840s a 60" engine was put on sale. The mine had 133 employees in 1847, but was working only above adit level. For most of the 19th century only "a little tin was got from time to time by tributers" (Collins). During the 1870s and 1880s Wheal Coates was worked on a larger scale, and it was then that most of the surviving structures were built, but it was not a particularly successful mine, producing only just over a thousand tons of ore, mainly tin, between 1815 and 1889, with another short period of working just before the First World War. The lower house, on Towanroath Shaft, contained the 30-inch pumping engine. This building was restored by the National Trust in 1973, and the stamps engine house above in 1986-8. The site as a whole is relatively complex and difficult to understand; if you are keen to learn more, I recommend the detailed study by the Cornwall Archaeological Unit: see the Further Reading section. At low tide it is worth going down to the beach (from Chapel Porth) to see the lode in the cliff-face and, if the tide is right and you are equipped with a torch, to explore the cave, at the back of which water still issues from the mouth of the adit. The lode has been extensively stoped in the roof of the cave.

Now walk on to Chapel Porth by the upper or lower tracks.

❹ If you haven't already explored Chapel Porth beach and its caves, it's well worth doing so, especially if the tide is low; see the details in the note on Wheal Coates, and also in section 8 of the directions for Walk 8 (page 69). In that case, walk up the road afterwards to the higher footbridge; but **if you don't want to go down to the beach, keep to the path above, which runs inland. Soon this descends to the road. Walk up the road and then take the track on the right down to a footbridge; cross this and turn left up Chapel Coombe (*).**

CHAPEL PORTH AND CHAPEL COOMBE

The site of "St Agnes Well and Chapel" has been identified on the north side of the cove, and according to a booklet published in 1979 by the Cornwall County Council, "Chapel Porth Nature Trail", a small chapel was dismantled in 1780. The valley was intensively mined from early times, and mine buildings occupied the area which is now the National Trust car park: see the photograph dated 1908 on page 19 of Clive Benney's earlier book. These, and the remains of buildings, leats and capped shafts further up the Coombe, were workings of mines called Charlotte United, East Charlotte and Wheal Freedom. To quote from the Nature Trail booklet, now regretably out of print,"Most of the noise in the valley" (that is, while the mines were working) "was caused by the tin crushing machines or 'stamps' which pounded the ore produced by local mines into fine sand. The crushing 'heads' of the stamps were raised by water power. Artificial cuttings or 'leats' channelled the water on to large water wheels. Stream water was supplemented by thousands of gallons pumped up from the lower levels of the mines by the great Cornish Beam engines housed in the weather and time resistant buildings still seen at the head of the valley."

Notice the various shafts and ruinous buildings in the valley. The engine house ahead contained a 30-inch pumping engine and belonged to a mine named on the late 19th-century maps as Charlotte United, though it had started in about 1806 as North Towan, and during its most productive period (c.1830-56) was called New Charlotte. It output was mostly copper. As you cross the wooden footbridge below it, look down to see the mouth of the mine's adit, now flooded. It is worth scrambling up the path just beyond for a closer look at the engine house, impressively sited against the backdrop of the valley down to the sea; but there are several deep pits around it, so great care is needed. **Continue along the valley path.**

Ruins of mine buildings in Chapel Coombe.
The engine house of Charlotte United is in the distance.

❺ After about 250 yards turn left, crossing two streams. Bear right on the main track, and where this bends left, keep right (almost, in fact, straight ahead). This track follows a stream, and passes below the dumps of another mine, called East Charlotte. This, together with the neighbouring Wheal Freedom, seems to have worked intermittently over a long period: there are records of sales of small amounts of copper in the 1820s and 1860s and a little tin early this century. Now, when you reach a charming old house set in a superb garden, suddenly the valley becomes idyllically rural and sheltered, filled with water-sounds and wild flowers: when my wife and I walked there last, quite early in March, there were already dozens of bluebells in full bloom. You may well be glad of waterproof footwear here: in March, the path itself was one of the streams! Many locals know this little valley as Wheal Lawrence, an interesting corruption of an old name: a spring here was called Venton Aurance, "Silver Spring", so the valley became Arrance Coombe and an old mine here was named Wheal Arrans - thus Lawrence was born. (Thanks to Bill Morrison for that information, which I culled from the 1986 Journal of the St Agnes Museum Trust.) **After passing through a gate, keep to the left of the field and cross the stile on the left by a wooden gate. Go up this track, turn left at the T-junction, and continue straight ahead across the road, going past a greenhouse and along a narrow path by a fence till you reach another road.**

❻ Turn left and immediately right up a track. Soon you fork left on to a narrower path which goes to the top of St Agnes Beacon (*). As you go, look right to see, on the skyline, Carn Brea crowned with the Basset monument; Carn Marth, the furthest left of the four hills; the woods near Scorrier to the left of that, and further left still the prominent engine house of North Treskerby. On the far right are Trencrom and the other hills south and west of St Ives. When you reach the trig. point at the top you will, in clear conditions, have a good view of the St Austell china-clay mining area in the east, and the coast as far as Trevose Head, near Padstow. Close at hand are the St Agnes mines, including Polberro on the cliff-edge and Wheal Kitty just beyond the village. Almost due east about five miles away is West Chiverton (Walk 2), but you will probably need binoculars or a vivid imagination to make it out. If you see East Wheal Rose, let me know!

The Beacon dominates the skyline as you approach St Agnes from Truro.
In the foreground on the left is part of the disused railway line.

WALK 10

ST AGNES BEACON

St Agnes Beacon - *"a stupendous and amazing high mountain"* in the eyes of William Hals (1655-1737) - is like a great island of killas (sedimentary rock) standing above the granite. At or near its top, 630 feet above sea level, are ancient burial mounds. The fact that an earthwork over 3km in length was constructed on the southern side of the hill - apparently linking Chapel Coombe and Trevaunance Coombe - suggests that the area it enclosed had some kind of special importance at one time. The earthwork, part of which has survived to a height of about 11ft from the bottom of the ditch to the top of the rampart, is now known as the Bolster Bank; *"Bolster"* seems to derive from Cornish words meaning *"a hump shaped like a boat"*. Other names it has been given include Kledh, meaning *"dyke"*, and Gorres, meaning *"weir, dam"*. If you are interested to know more about it, see the article by Nicholas Johnson in *"Cornish Archaeology"* No. 19 (1980). The purpose of the earthwork and the date of its construction remain matters for speculation. All around the hill, near the top, is a layer of grey clay, used by the early miners to attach tallow candles to their helmets (and I suppose this is the same clay which Thomas Tonkin says was *"much used by pipe makers")*, and beneath this clay is a stratum of sand and pebbles, showing that millions of years ago the sea must have been at this level, or that earth-movements have lifted the rocks - or that this is the high-tide mark of Noah's Flood, as the old miners apparently held. (Perhaps they got the idea from Tonkin, who wrote that it is *"clear evidence of the Deluge".)* The clay and sand have both been quarried in recent years, mainly for use in iron foundries. Remains of openwork tin mining, and also stone quarries which supplied the building material for the engine houses, can also be found on the Beacon. The hill has been quarried in a small way for centuries, and the family doing the quarrying now have been involved for over 150 years. From the top of St Agnes Beacon can be seen, it is claimed, 30 church towers, as well as ships at anchor in Falmouth Bay, and the top of St Michael's Mount: a perfect site for the beacon fires lit in times of emergency or rejoicing. Even Carn Brea, Carn Marth, Trencrom and Carn Galver cannot beat it as a place to stand and reflect on Cornwall's industrial past, and what its future may hold.

From the trig. point, take the path leading down towards St Agnes; it curves left and right before reaching a road.

❼ Turn left. Just past the group of houses, turn right over a stile by a public footpath sign. For a short distance, keep by the wall on your left; then cross the stile on your right, and head for the group of engine houses and stacks. After two more stiles, the path runs between hedges. After that, keep by the hedge on the left to another stile by a gate, and continue ahead on the wide track. At the road, go straight on down the path, to emerge near the church on the main street. Turn right to return to the car park.

SOME MINING TERMS USED IN THIS BOOK

(Unless otherwise stated, the quotations are from "A History of the Parish of Gwennap", by C. C. James)

ADIT A drainage channel with its mouth or "portal" in a valley or on a hillside or cliff face. In deep mines, the water had to be raised by pumping to the level of the adit; this is why statistics often state the depth of a mine "below adit". Adits also often doubled as shafts by following the metal lode, and provided access for the miners.

BEAM ENGINE Thomas Newcomen of Dartmouth (1663-1729) was the first to develop a steam engine which could be used for pumping water up from mines. The cylinder was placed vertically, and the piston was chained to one end of a massive wooden or cast iron beam, pivoted on a strong wall. The other end overhung the mine shaft and was attached by long rods to the pump at the bottom. In the 1770s James Watt and Matthew Boulton began manufacturing an improved version, and James Pickard modified beam engines to produce rotative motion, used mainly for winding and driving the stamps. Early in the 19th century, great improvements were brought by the use of high-pressure steam as a result of the research and inventions of Richard Trevithick (1771-1833). Pages 6 to 9 of the Illustrated Catalogue published by Williams' Perran Foundry in the late 1870s and re-issued by the Trevithick Society in 1986 have good drawings of several types of beam engine. The dimension, expressed in inches, given in this book against many of the engines is the cylinder bore, a figure used in Cornwall to denote the power of an engine, as opposed to using a horsepower rating.

BLOWING HOUSE The early form of smelting house, in which the furnace temperature was raised by bellows, usually operated by a waterwheel.

BOB WALL This was the strongest wall of an engine house, which supported the bob or beam of the engine.

BUDDLE The earliest buddles were rectangular pits; according to James, "stamped tin is curiously washed from its impurities by water constantly running through the buddles, while a boy is standing in it working with a shovel and also with his feet". By 1850, convex round buddles about 20 feet across had come into use; the slime containing the crushed ore was fed in at the centre, and rotating brushes swept the lightest material to the edges, leaving the metal near the centre. Concave buddles were used for finer material.

BURNING HOUSE A furnace or **CALCINER** (pronounced "cal-*sign*-er") where tin was made red-hot in order to burn off impurities such as sulphur and arsenic. If the arsenic was wanted, the fumes were passed through a

92

long, zigzag flue known as a **LAMBRETH** (labyrinth), from which the deposits were collected.

BURROW Waste tip.

CALCINER See BURNING HOUSE.

COFFIN, COFFEN or **GOFFEN** One of many terms used for mining on surface. A coffin or **GUNNIS** is a narrow, slot-like excavation; where a broader, quarry-like pit was dug the term was **OPENWORK** or **BEAM**. The word **STOPE** normally means an excavated area underground, but is also sometimes used of surface workings.

COUNT HOUSE The mine's office.

DRESSING FLOOR The area where the large lumps of ore were broken up manually, often by boys and "bal maidens", fed to the stamping machines and finally treated in the buddles before the metal was smelted.

DRIVE A horizontal tunnel.

FATHOM Six feet, as in nautical terminology.

FLAT-RODS Wooden or iron rods which were used to transfer power from an engine to a remote location.

GANGUE The unwanted materials in the ore.

GUNNIS See COFFIN.

HALVANS Poor quality ore.

KINGPOST This was sometimes used along with "bridles" to add strength to the beam in a Cornish engine - necessary with the early wooden beams. The top of the kingpost also made a convenient point for flat-rods to be linked to an engine.

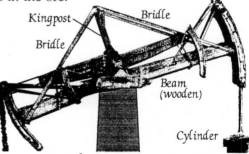

Part of a Newcomen engine, c.1760

LAMBRETH See BURNING HOUSE.

LEVEL "A tunnel connecting the shaft with the lode."

LODE "Any vein that appears likely to produce metallic ore."

OLD MEN'S SHAFTS / WORKINGS This refers to mines or openwork pits which pre-date existing records; this usually means, before the mid-18th century.

SETT "The ground granted to a company of adventurers." The same term is also used to refer to stone railway or tramway sleepers.

STAMPS Cornish Stamps machines were used to crush the small lumps of ore into material like sand in texture. Heavy timber or iron lifters with iron "heads" at the bottom were raised by cams on a rotating axle, and fell on the ore, fed into a box beneath. Small stamps were usually powered by waterwheels and larger ones by steam engines. The Perran Foundry catalogue (see BEAM ENGINE) illustrates stamps on page 12; see also page 69 in this book.

STOPE   See COFFIN.

STREAMING   The normal method of winning tin before deep mining became possible, and practised in recent times in several places, such as the Bissoe valley, and on a small scale at the seaward end of Trevellas Coombe. Tin washed down into valleys and buried under layers of silt was exposed, originally by shovel and wheelbarrow; the tin-bearing gravel was then sorted and washed, and the waste material used to back-fill the excavated area. Nowadays, earth-movers and lorries take that same material to plants where modern methods are able to extract the valuable minerals still present.

TAILINGS DAM   In modern tin mines, the waste material, mixed with water, is pumped into a dam and allowed to settle; eventually the water may be re-used by the mine, and the tailings are sometimes re-processed at a later date when higher prices or improved technology make this worthwhile. Finally - at least in theory - the dried-out dam is grassed over.

TRIBUTER   A miner who contracted to work for a limited time.   (The Cornish miners prided themselves on their independence, and were reluctant to become mere employees.)

WHIM   A machine for raising water, ore or other heavy materials from the mine. The earliest whims were operated by horses, which walked round and round turning a wooden drum around which was wound the cable attached to the "kibble" or bucket. Horse whims continued in use by small mines until quite recent times: my drawing is of one being used by tributers at Polberro mine about 1907. The whims in deep mines were driven by steam engines, and in the early 19th century these were sometimes known as "fire whims".

WINZE   "A small ventilating shaft between two levels" (Chambers) Winzes were also sometimes used for access.

Horse whim, Polberro

FURTHER READING

Several of these books are out of print, but most can be obtained through public libraries.

ACTON, BOB — *A View from Carn Brea, A Second View from Carn Marth, Around Newquay, Around the River Fowey* and *Around St Austell* are the volumes in the Landfall Walks Books series that most closely relate to historical details in this book.

ATKINSON, BARRY — *Mining Sites in Cornwall and South-West Devon* (Dyllansow Truran, 1988)

ATKINSON, R. L. — *Tin and Tin Streaming* (Shire Publications,1988)

BENNETT, ALAN — *Images of Cornwall* (Runpast Publishing,1992)

BENNEY, CLIVE — *St Agnes Parish, 1850-1920* (Clive Benney / Diversions Ltd, no date)

BENNEY, CLIVE — *St Agnes Parish, 1920-1950* (Clive Benney, 1988)

BIRD, R. H. — *Britain's Old Metal Mines* (Moorland Publishing)

BIZLEY, M.H. — *Friendly Retreat: The Story of a Parish* (1955; to be reprinted by the St Agnes Museum Trust, 1994)

BIZLEY, M.H. — *A Portrait of a Village Church: The Parish Church of Saint Agnes, in the County of Cornwall, England* (Original now scarce, but a typed transcript may be available in the church)

BUCKLEY, J.A. — *Cornish Mining - at Surface* (Tor Mark Press, 1990)

COLLINS, J. H. — *Observations on the West of England Mining Region* (1912; Cornish Mining Classics, 1988)

CORNWALL FEDERATION OF WOMEN'S INSTITUTES — *The Cornwall Village Book* (Countryside Books, 1991)

DOUCH, H. L. — *East Wheal Rose* (Bradford Barton, 1964)

HATTAM, DEREK — *Cornish Land Steam in and around Perran Parish* (Dyllansow Truran, 1983)

HENWOOD, GEORGE — *Cornwall's Mines and Miners* (1857-9; Bradford Barton 1972)

JENKIN, A. K. H. — *The Mines and Miners of Cornwall* (c.1960-70; most recent edition by Forge Books)
Volume 2: St Agnes to Perranporth
Volume 7: Perranporth to Newquay

JOHN, C.R. — *The Saints of Cornwall* (Dyllansow Truran, 1981)

Further Reading

KING, JOHN — *The Parish of St Agnes, Cornwall* (typewritten pamphlet - may be available in the church)

LAWS, PETER — *Cornish Engines* (The National Trust, 1993)

NOALL, CYRIL — *Cornish Mine Disasters* (Dyllansow Truran, 1989)

ORDISH, H. G. — *Cornish Engine Houses, A Pictorial Survey* (Bradford Barton, 1967)

ORDISH, H. G. — *Cornish Engine Houses, A Second Pictorial Survey* (Bradford Barton, 1968)

PADEL, O.J. — *Cornish Place-Name Elements* (English Place-Name Society, 1985)

PADEL, O.J. — *A Popular Dictionary of Cornish Place-Names* (Alison Hodge, 1988)

PEARCE, FRANK — *Portrait of a Cornish Village: St Agnes* (Bantam Books, 1977)

PERRANZABULOE OLD CORNWALL SOCIETY — *Perran Paths* (Penwartha Press, no date)

READE, LEWIS — *Branch Line Memories, Volume 1: Great Western* (Atlantic, 1983)

READE, LEWIS — *The Branch Lines of Cornwall* (Atlantic, 1984)

SHARPE, ADAM and SMITH, JOHN R. — *Trevellas, St Agnes*
Wheal Coates, St Agnes
(Two reports produced by the Cornwall Archaeological Unit in 1986)

ST AGNES MUSEUM TRUST — Annual Journals, from 1984
St Agnes Miners' & Mechanics' Institute, 1893-1993

STANIER, PETER — *Cornwall's Mining Heritage* (Twelveheads Press, 1988)

STENGELHOFEN, JOHN — *Cornwall's Railway Heritage* (Twelveheads Press, 1988)

TANNER, KATHY — *St Agnes and Chapel Porth* (National Trust "Coast of Cornwall" leaflet No. 8, 1987)

TOMLIN, E.W.F. — *In Search of St Piran* (Lodenek Press, 1982)

TONKIN, THOMAS — *The Parish of St Agnes* (written c.1710-33, reprinted in the Journal of the Royal Institution of Cornwall, 1975-6)

TREMBATH, BILL — *Perranporth and Perranzabuloe Parish* (Lodenek Press, 1992)

TROUNSON, J. — *Mining in Cornwall*, Volume 2 (Moorland, n.d.)

WILLIAMS, H. V. — *Cornwall's Old Mines* (Tor Mark Press, n.d.)